The Quotable Henry Ford

UNIVERSITY PRESS OF FLORIDA

Florida A&M University, Tallahassee
Florida Atlantic University, Boca Raton
Florida Gulf Coast University, Ft. Myers
Florida International University, Miami
Florida State University, Tallahassee
New College of Florida, Sarasota
University of Central Florida, Orlando
University of Florida, Gainesville
University of North Florida, Jacksonville
University of South Florida, Tampa
University of West Florida, Pensacola

The Quotable
Henry Ford

Edited by
Michele Wehrwein Albion

Foreword by Howard P. Segal

University Press of Florida

Gainesville/Tallahassee/Tampa/Boca Raton/Pensacola
Orlando/Miami/Jacksonville/Ft. Myers/Sarasota

18 17 16 15 14 13   6 5 4 3 2 1

Library of Congress Cataloging-in-Publication Data
Ford, Henry, 1863–1947.
The quotable Henry Ford / edited by Michele Wehrwein Albion;
foreword by Howard P. Segal.
p. cm.
Includes bibliographical references and index.
ISBN 978-0-8130-4405-7 (alk. paper)
1. Ford, Henry, 1863–1947—Quotations. I. Albion, Michele Wehrwein.
II. Segal, Howard P. III. Title.
TL140.F6F665 2012
081—dc23
2012031970

Previous page: Henry Ford, January 1916. Courtesy of the Library
of Congress, LC-USZ62-62286.

University Press of Florida
15 Northwest 15th Street
Gainesville, FL 32611-2079
http://www.upf.com

For my parents,
Marjorie Marcotte
and Gregory Wehrwein,
and my bonus parents,
Ann Ogilvie Wehrwein
and James Benson

Contents

Foreword   ix

Preface and Acknowledgments   xv

Chronology   xxiii

1 On Automobiles, Tractors, and Other Transportation Technology   1

2 On the Ford Motor Company, Business, and Management   11

3 On Money and Economics   28

4 On Employees and Ford's Social Policies   39

5 On Work and Leisure   54

6 On Machines and Technology   63

7 On Politics and Government   68

8 On War and Peace   78

9 On Law, the Legal System, Crime and Punishment   89

10 On Education and the Arts   94

11 On History, the Past, and Museums 101

12 On the Press 107

13 On Humanity 110

14 On Religion, Reincarnation, and Charity 120

15 On Nations, Nationalities, Ethnic and Religious Groups, and the United States 131

16 On Health 142

17 On Nature, Science, Energy, and Fuel 150

18 On Family 158

19 On Himself 163

20 On Miscellaneous Topics 169

21 Henry Ford on Others 191

22 Others on Henry Ford 197

Notes 213

Bibliography 257

Foreword

Michele Albion deserves much praise for putting together this book. Despite the countless volumes published over the years about Henry Ford, there is none like hers. Although Ford died in 1947, *The Quotable Henry Ford* is, if anything, more valuable today than when Henry was alive. For many Americans, Henry remains an admired, even beloved, figure. When American manufacturers are commonly criticized for moving so many facilities and products abroad, Henry is often held up as a great manufacturer who never neglected his home base despite establishing an international corporation with plants in many other countries. The fact that Henry and his children, grandchildren, and great-grandchildren still exercise considerable power over the company as stockholders makes the corporation's continued commitment to the United States and to its Michigan roots much appreciated.

To be sure, Henry remains a controversial figure in American history still despised by many for his controversial opinions on any number of subjects, from labor unions to industrial cities to Jews. It is indicative of Henry's mixed reputation that not until the late 1990s and early 2000s, when the Ford Motor Company was temporarily headed by his great-grandson, William Clay Ford Jr., that advertisements and commercials invoking the company's founder were finally used. These promotions, moreover, praised

Henry for his pioneering environmental vision and were not expected to revive any dormant ill feelings toward the company.

Still, as Michele Albion acknowledges, previous scholars who have studied Henry for years still cannot completely understand him. So why try to pin down his views on a variety of topics? For that matter, given Henry's pronounced lack of systematic thinking on nearly all subjects, plus his lack of much formal education, why try to reconstruct his sometimes contradictory as well as controversial views? Precisely because Henry was a folk hero to millions of Americans—and many non-Americans—for decades. Like Thomas Edison, whose views were illuminated in Albion's complementary volume, *The Quotable Edison*, Henry was widely viewed as a man of exceptional wisdom for decades even when he clearly lacked any expertise about most of the non-business topics on which he was persistently asked his opinion.

It is hard to imagine any highly successful businessperson today being put on the pedestals that both Henry and Edison occupied for so long. The handful of contemporary entrepreneurs who have become household names—Bill Gates, Warren Buffett, and the late Steve Jobs above all—have been accorded recognition primarily for their technical and financial achievements and, in the case of Gates, for establishing charitable organizations that do not pretend to reflect any expertise on Gates's part in, say, medicine and public health in third world countries.

Henry's intellectual weaknesses extended to his limited speaking and writing skills. Albion notes his difficulties in speaking and writing coherently, but his written communications, as described by the economist John Kenneth Galbraith in a 1958 essay, were even worse than his oral communications. Having examined surviving samples of Ford's own unedited writings, the late great Harvard economist characterized them as almost impossible to decipher. See Galbraith, "Was Ford a Fraud?" reprinted in his *The*

Liberal Hour (Boston: Houghton Mifflin, 1960), 141–165. Albion addresses this issue and handles it well.

Interestingly, the traditional American deference to entertainment and sports figures for their views on issues outside of their respective realms of knowledge and experience still persists. Many of these celebrities have good intentions, and their ability to generate publicity for various humanitarian causes offsets the envy, if not the resentment, that many outsiders may feel. Yet whenever these celebrities leave their comparatively safe stages, studios, and playing fields for other public arenas, they risk the exposure as non-experts—and possibly fools—that so often undermined Henry's positive public image. It proved harmful to that once-glowing image when Henry praised the Great Depression as a valuable cleansing agent for the American economy; and when Ford continued to demonize labor unions for the four years after the United Auto Workers finally reached agreements with Ford Motor Company's principal rivals, General Motors and Chrysler, in 1937. Worse yet for many Americans and non-Americans was Ford's anti-Semitism, as espoused in his *Dearborn Independent*. Once Henry belatedly recognized the damage caused by his hatred of Jews to his sales as well as to his reputation, he nevertheless blamed others for newspaper editorials and other publications. Albion handles this issue with sensitivity and professionalism.

Yet one cannot forget that in the 1910s Henry had a very close friend and Detroit neighbor, Rabbi Leo Franklin, who, in 1920, was shocked to read the initial anti-Semitic *Dearborn Independent* articles. Rabbi Franklin returned to Ford the Model T that had been given him as a mark of their close relationship. When in 1927 Ford retracted his bigoted writings, Franklin reconciled with Ford, by now living in his palatial Dearborn estate. Few other American Jews, however, were so forgiving.

One also cannot ignore the fact that Albert Kahn, the principal industrial architect of Ford Motor Company's most important plants (first Highland Park and then the gigantic Rouge), roughly 1000 conventional plants worldwide, and several of the nineteen Ford village industries that I wrote about, was Jewish and that Henry helped elevate him into the foremost such American architect of his time. Moreover, Kahn designed and built several Ford family homes. Not only was Kahn, the son of a German rabbi, commonly described as "Henry Ford's architect," but Henry gave an effusive eulogy at Kahn's funeral in 1942. Henry, then, epitomized the old line that "some of my best friends are Jews."

Similarly, Henry mirrored the racist beliefs of many of his fellow white Americans that black Americans were inferior intellectually and perhaps in other respects. Yet he insisted that the Ford Motor Company hire roughly the same percentage of African American workers in at least its Detroit and Detroit-area factories as were in the general population of the region: ten percent. True, African American workers at Ford Motor Company were given the worst and most dangerous jobs, as in the paint shops. But, by contrast, General Motors and Chrysler hired virtually no African Americans. Meanwhile Henry befriended the distinguished scientist George Washington Carver at Tuskegee Institute in Alabama and provided financial support for Carver's agricultural research that so intrigued Henry. Both men believed that peanuts, soybeans, and other agricultural products could be converted into plastics, paint, fuel, and additional industrial products. Henry also donated funds to improve Carver's lab and to install an elevator for use during the scientist's later years. In addition, Henry had reconstructed in Greenfield Village a replica of the log cabin where Carver was born into slavery into Missouri.

How can one reconcile such contradictions? One cannot, of course, readily or fully do so, and it is probable that Henry himself never completely grasped what, to many others, was painfully obvious. The famous lines from Walt Whitman's "Song of Myself" come to mind: "Do I contradict myself? Very well then, I contradict myself. (I am large. I contain multitudes.)"

I myself came to appreciate Henry's complexity when, having been appointed to the University of Michigan in 1978 to teach the history of technology to students in its College of Engineering, I spent many days at the Henry Ford Museum and Greenfield Village (now collectively called The Henry Ford), trying to understand him and his legacy. I eventually concentrated on two other examples of his contradictory impulses and values: his dislike of farming dating to his youth on a Dearborn farm and his later insistence that all of his workers be part-time farmers; and his desire to depopulate Detroit and other large American industrial and manufacturing cities that he had done so much to increase in size through his auto production facilities and related businesses. I came to focus upon Henry's nineteen village industries that were located within a sixty-mile radius of Dearborn. As detailed in my book, *Recasting the Machine Age: Henry Ford's Village Industries*, I became fascinated by Henry's conflicting attitudes toward modernity. Here as elsewhere, he was at once looking ahead and looking backward. Unlike most of us, Henry had the means of trying to fulfill both impulses, and in ways that can still be appreciated in the twentieth-first century.

I hope that *The Quotable Henry Ford* will enlighten many readers about the complexities of this seemingly simple man. I thank Michele Albion for this wonderful contribution to our understanding of Henry Ford.

Howard P. Segal

Preface and
Acknowledgments

Upon learning that his friend Henry Ford was considering a run for president, Thomas Edison was flummoxed. "What do you want to do that for? You can't speak. You wouldn't say a damned word. You'd be mum."[1] He was right. Ford was a stammering, tongue-tied, and largely inept public speaker. "You know I don't make speeches; I make cars," he later declared.[2]

Though no orator, Ford still had plenty to say. After the Model T made him famous, the automobile manufacturer began to see himself as a philosopher in the vein of Ben Franklin or Ralph Waldo Emerson. He kept notebooks of comments and pithy sayings, reworking them to get the wording just right—even if the spelling or grammar was not.

As Ford became even more renowned, an eager public hung on his every syllable, hoping they too would discover the key to wealth and fame. One reporter, comparing him to Sophocles, observed: "He is steadily pelted away at, with request for an opinion, as the oracle of Delphi. Anything he says, while stopping in one town to change trains, or in another town to change tires, is promptly put on the wire and reported to ten thousand newspapers."[3]

Ford reveled in the media attention. Though he was skeptical about the value of advertising automobiles, he had no problem devoting company resources to promoting himself. In books, newspapers, and magazine articles, Ford and his staff carefully crafted his image as a folksy, plainspoken visionary who cared about the plight of the common man.

The media, for its part, was eager to publish feature stories on the automobile magnate. Though articles about Henry Ford guaranteed bylines, obtaining interviews was often challenging. Ford's executive staff—which included numerous bodyguards, such as the tenacious Ernest G. Liebold and former navy boxer Harry Bennett—often proved to be a barrier.

Should a reporter actually succeed in obtaining a face-to-face interview with Ford, his communication style presented the next hurdle. Today Ford might be labeled as having an attention deficit disorder. His secretary, Louis Lochner, observed that Ford's mind "jumps from one thing to another, so that we have quite a job to hold him to the thing at hand."[4] Many times a reporter walked away wondering how he or she could possibly piece together a stream of scattered—and sometimes bizarre—pronouncements into a coherent article. Often Ford's staff would explain, "What Mr. Ford meant was . . ."[5]

Henry Ford was a bundle of contradictions packaged in a soybean suit.[6] In some ways, Ford was a simple, homespun man. He enjoyed bird-watching, square dancing, and spending quiet evenings at home with his wife. In other ways he was ahead of his time. He supported women's suffrage and complained that women were not given enough credit for their work in the home. He employed African Americans and the handicapped, believing that all people deserved the right to work.

He was all those things, but in time, the phenomenal growth of the Ford Motor Company and his personal wealth transformed Henry Ford into something else. He was a millionaire, then billionaire, who lived in a mansion. With his labor policies, large-scale factories, and assembly lines, Ford not only changed the nature of work but created a new means of controlling the fates of employees. At times his decisions affected not only the Ford Motor Company but also the entire automotive industry. Sometimes his actions influenced national and international economies.

Despite his own statements about the triviality of money, Ford discussed it constantly and used his fortune to alter society. He saw each of his revolutionary management policies—the five-dollar day, eight-hour day, and five-day week—as a tool to induce his employees and their families to better living.

Though Ford claimed "paternalism has no place in industry,"[7] he established a "Sociological Department" to monitor his employees' behavior on and off the clock. Drinking alcohol, allowing wives to work, taking in male boarders, and imprudent use of wages made workers ineligible for higher pay or could result in their termination.

Adding to the power of his purse was the fact that by the 1920s, almost inexplicably, Henry Ford had developed a fervent belief in reincarnation. Suddenly his personal fame, success, and wealth were not an anomaly. Instead, they represented the hard-earned result of, and the reward for, his hard work in previous lives. With that reward came a responsibility to attain even greater achievements in the next life by doing good in this one. He explained:

> We are here to work out something, and we go on from where we leave off. That's my religion, though I was brought up an Episcopalian. For myself, I'm certain that I have lived before, that I stored up considerable experience before the present stage, and that I will proceed to the next stage when this is finished.[8]

If personal responsibility and the promise of a better future life were not enough, Henry Ford also sought to emulate his idol, Thomas Edison. By the time they became friends, the world's most famous inventor was celebrated for witticisms such as, "Genius is one per cent inspiration, ninety-nine per cent perspiration."[9] Ford hoped to achieve the same iconic status.

Ford commented on a variety of topics. He discussed automobiles, of course, but also war, literature, dancing, obesity, and his assertion that overalls were not appropriate attire for women. While some of his comments are charming or witty and famously quotable, others are offensive and *infamously* quotable.

Henry Ford was an anti-Semite. Historians have linked his hatred of Jews to his childhood reading material as well as the widespread bigotry pervasive during his time. Neither begins to explain the depth of his paranoia and hatred of Jews. He fervently believed Jews were part of a conspiracy to achieve worldwide domination, and his *Dearborn Independent* published the "Protocols of the Learned Elders of Zion" in serial form, which purported to confirm his theory. Ford was undeterred by the fact that the publication was a well-documented hoax.

Originally I intended to include Ford's anti-Semitic statements in this book of quotations because, as offensive as they are, they represent Ford's thoughts and beliefs. It soon became evident, however, that he made not a few, but hundreds of anti-Semitic comments. Rather than allow this book to become a resource for racists, the section on Jews in chapter 15 is in narrative form, placing Ford's comments and actions in the historical context of his life.

It should be noted that anti-Semitism was not uncommon in the United States during Ford's lifetime. Jews were often excluded from fraternal organizations and social clubs, unofficially banned from certain professions, subjected to restrictive quotas in higher education, and sometimes prohibited from purchasing property. But anti-Semitic comments coming from someone as famous as Henry Ford had the potential to influence many others.

Whether or not it was Ford's intent, Nazi Germany used his pronouncements and propaganda as justification for the persecution of Jews during World War II. Thus, through his anti-Semitic statements and racist publications, Henry Ford contributed to the wholesale extermination of men, women, and children.

Comments Henry Ford made about other nationalities have been maintained in their original form. Some are offensive and reflect the limitations of his character.

Historical events, economic conditions, and political movements influenced Henry Ford. Where these elements are not self-evident, brief background information is provided to help place these comments within a larger framework. Those seeking a deeper understanding will want to read one of the many excellent biographies of Henry Ford.

The quotes retain their original form and often include Henry Ford's mistakes in grammar and spelling. In some cases, spellings like "employe" represent common contemporary usage. Where press reports of the same event use slightly different language, it has been noted. Paraphrased quotes have not been included.

Since Ford was not a gifted speaker or writer, others in his employ transmitted his expressed thoughts onto the page. His autobiography, *My Life and Work*, and most articles credited to Ford during the 1920s were written by Samuel Crowther. Ford's stories in the *Dearborn Independent* were often the result of conversations with Ernest Liebold and William J. Cameron.

When his writings were received favorably, Ford tended to take credit. If taken to task for offensive statements, he blamed others. When he sued the *Chicago Tribune* for libel in 1919, Ford held his secretary, Theodore Delavigne, accountable for portraying him as an isolationist. Later, during the Sapiro trial, Ford claimed Cameron was solely responsible for the publication's anti-Semitic articles.

Sometimes it is difficult to ascertain what Ford said and what was expressed in his name by others. For the purposes of this book, anything that was presented by an individual in his employ and publicly credited to Henry Ford will be considered his own. Attribution becomes especially nebulous with Henry Ford's own newspaper, the *Dearborn Independent*. Although Ford likely initiated most of the newspaper's content, only those on "Mr. Ford's Page" have been included.

Likely there were times when reporters misquoted or misunderstood Ford's comments. Where Ford publicly denied a statement, it has been noted.

Quotations for this book were selected based on three criteria: statements for which Ford is either famous or infamous; quotes with historical or cultural significance that place Henry Ford in the context of his life and times; and comments the industrialist made on topics regarding his own interests.

Henry Ford's recorded comments do not necessarily represent every facet of his life. Though he cared a great deal about birds and the natural environment, he said little about them publicly. The documented statements about his son, Edsel, do not begin to convey the complexity of their relationship.

Further, because of the sheer quantity of comments Ford uttered over his long life, repetitive quotes or nuanced versions of previous quotes have been omitted. When possible, endnotes cite similar statements.

Numerous sources were scoured in the process of compiling this book. They include publications authored and coauthored by Henry Ford, his autobiographies, and numerous biographies of him and of family members, company executives, and friends. Further, I consulted many Ford Motor Company publications and industrial histories. The most fruitful sources were often contemporary newspapers and magazine articles.

Though the sources are quite varied, undoubtedly many worthy quotes have been overlooked, and others wait to be discovered. Many statements attributed to the automaker have been excluded because no primary source of the document has been located. For example, "A bore is a person who opens his mouth and puts his feats in it," may have been uttered by Ford. Because it cannot be documented at this time, it has not been included in this edition.

I hope this will be the first step in a continuing effort to compile Ford's quotations. Readers are invited to send additional quotes with citations to: Ford's Quotations, PO Box 487, Dover, NH 03821, or via www.michelealbion.com.

Henry Ford is a difficult man to understand. Historian and Ford biographer David L. Lewis said, "I probably know more about Ford's life and work than any other writer. But I cannot say that I have completely sorted him out, nor am I sure that I shall fully understand him."[10] This book does not purport to provide a definitive understanding of Ford's personality or character. However, it is hoped that *The Quotable Henry Ford* will provide a glimpse into a man who helped to shape the twentieth century.

I would like to thank a number of people who helped make this book possible. I cannot say enough about the great talents and nearly unlimited patience of librarians. Thank you to Sue Vincent of the Dover Public Library; Peggy O'Kane, Dean Corner, and Marie Pierce of the Maine State Library; Mel Johnson, social sciences and humanities reference librarian at the University of Maine's Fogler Library; Deanna Wood and Nicole Hentz at the University of New Hampshire's Dimond Library; and Duane Shaffer, fellow author and head of collections development and adult programs at the Sanibel Public Library, Sanibel, Florida.

Thanks also to the National Archives, especially Jessica Kratz from the Center for Legislative Archives; the Edison National

Historic Park, specifically Leonard DeGraaf, for offering access to the wonderful photographs and images shared to create this book.

Last, but by no means least, thank you to the staff of, and consultants to, the University Press of Florida. Special thanks to freelance editor Susan Murray, to Associate Director and Editor-in-Chief Amy Gorelick, and Assistant Editor Sonia Dickey for your patience and support.

Prior to editing, this manuscript draft contained more than seven hundred single-spaced pages of Henry Ford quotes. Marjorie Marcotte, Pamela Oberg, Beth Tykodi, and Bodhipaksa all kindly assisted in the preliminary selection process. Further thanks go to David Lucsko, assistant professor in the History Department at Auburn University, who shared his valuable insight and expertise.

Chronology

July 30, 1863	Henry Ford is born in Greenfield Township, Wayne County, Michigan, to William and Mary Litogot Ford.
1876	His mother, Mary Litogot Ford, dies.
1879	Works in machine shops and at the Michigan Car Company in Detroit.
1880	Becomes a machine apprentice and repairs watches in his spare time.
1882	Repairs steam-driven farm machinery and works as a steam-engine operator at the Westinghouse company.
1884–85	Attends business school in Detroit.
1888	Marries Clara Jane Bryant and moves to Dearborn.
1891	Serves as an engineer at the Edison Illuminating Company in Detroit.
1893	Son Edsel is born. Becomes chief engineer at the Edison Illuminating Company. In his off hours, experiments with a homemade internal combustion engine.
June 4, 1896	Builds and tests his first car, the Ford Quadricyle. Meets Thomas Edison.

August 5, 1899	Establishes the Detroit Automobile Company and becomes chief engineer.
1901	The Detroit Automobile Company fails. Henry founds a new automobile venture, the Henry Ford Company.
1902	Race-car driver Barney Oldfield wins the Manufacturer's Challenge Cup driving Ford's automobile.
1903	Incorporates the Ford Motor Company and launches the Model A.
1907	His father, William Ford, dies.
October 1, 1908	The Model T is introduced.
1910	Builds an automobile plant in Highland Park, Michigan.
1911	Wins patent-infringement lawsuit against George Selden.
1913	Introduces the modern assembly line for mass production of his Ford automobiles. Opens plants in Canada and Britain.
1914	Establishes profit-sharing program with employees and the Five-Dollar Day.
1915	Finances and sails on the "Peace Ship" *Oscar II* to persuade leaders to stop war.
1917	Constructs the Rouge factory near the Rouge River in Dearborn.
1918	Asked by President Woodrow Wilson to run for the U.S. Senate. Fails to garner enough support at the Republican National Convention. Purchases the *Dearborn Independent* newspaper.

1919	His son, Edsel, becomes president of the Ford Motor Company, but Henry Ford continues to run the company.
1922–24	Ford's *Dearborn Independent* serializes "The Protocols of the Learned Elders of Zion," a known forged document purporting to detail a Jewish plan for world domination.
1926	Creates the Tri-Motor airplane.
1927	Model T production ends. The second Model A is launched at the River Rouge plant. The *Dearborn Independent* is shut down.
1929	Henry Ford Museum and Greenfield Village opens in Dearborn.
1932	Introduces V-8 engine for the Ford Model A. Artist Diego Rivera visits Ford in Dearborn.
1933	Refuses to cooperate with unions in Ford factories.
May 26, 1937	In what would be known as the Battle of the Overpass, Ford Motor Company security forces and United Auto Workers clash in a bloody altercation.
July 1938	Awarded the Grand Cross of the German Eagle, the highest honor awarded by the Nazi Party.
1941	Following a sit-down strike at the River Rouge plant, Ford signs a contract with United Autoworkers Union.
May 26, 1943	Edsel Ford dies at the age of forty-nine. Henry Ford resumes Ford Motor Company presidency.
1945	Grandson Henry Ford II assumes the presidency of the Ford Motor Company.
April 7, 1947	Henry Ford dies of cerebral hemorrhage at the age of eighty-three.

Henry Ford in his first model car. Courtesy of the New York Public Library, 9263. Photography Collection, Miriam and Ira D. Wallach Division of Art, Prints, and Photographs, New York Public Library, Astor, Lenox, and Tilden Foundations.

1 ⚙ On Automobiles, Tractors, and Other Transportation Technology

When the Ford Motor Company was founded in 1903, the automobile was an expensive toy owned by an elite few. Henry Ford thought automobiles should be a necessity, not a luxury—a tool to create a better life.

To achieve this, Ford simplified auto production. After five years of evolving Ford vehicles, from 1908 to 1927 he stuck to the Model T. The "flivver," or "Tin Lizzie" as it was called, was simple, durable, easy to repair, and inexpensive to maintain, making it popular with middle-class consumers. It came only in black because black paint dried the fastest. His Highland Park plant, located outside Detroit, employed new production methods. Through maximized efficiency of interchangeable parts and assembly lines, the Model T became the world's first mass-produced automobile and was soon selling at a rate of about 2 million annually.[1]

The Model T and other makes of automobiles altered the American landscape by creating the need for improved roads and highways. Middle-class Americans fled urban centers and moved to newly created suburbs. The automobile also spurred the economy with new businesses like gas stations, fast-food restaurants, and drive-in theaters.

The automobile made Henry Ford first a millionaire, then a billionaire. But by the early 1920s, the Ford Company was struggling. Ford sales declined 15 percent in 1924. The next year, General Motors outsold Ford because, while Ford stuck to one car, always black, General Motors produced new models that changed annually and came in a variety of colors and styles.[2]

Henry Ford resisted change for years but finally acquiesced in 1927 with the new Model A, which came in four colors—none of them black—had a 40-horsepower engine and seventeen body styles. The Model A was an immediate sensation, outselling Chevrolet by 34 percent in 1929.[3] More than 4 million Model A cars had been produced when production was halted in 1931.[4] In 1932, Henry Ford introduced the first V-8 engine in a mass-produced car.

Neither the Model A nor the powerful V-8 allowed the Ford Motor Company to regain its previous standing. The Great Depression, competition from Chrysler and Chevrolet, and Ford's disputes with unions all contributed to declining sales. Between 1930 and 1933, the Ford Motor Company lost an estimated $120 million[5] and laid off so many workers that company payroll was cut by over 75 percent.[6]

In addition to automobiles, Ford manufactured tractors beginning in 1917. During both world wars, Ford plants were mobilized to support the war effort. During World War II, Ford produced enough airplanes and automobiles to make it the nation's third-largest defense contractor.[7]

On Automobiles

What I would like to do is make an engine that will run by gasoline and have it do the work of a horse.[8]

Circa 1887–1902

The way to make automobiles is to make one automobile like another automobile, to make them all alike, to make them come through the factory just alike; just as one pin is like another pin when it comes from a pin factory, or one match is like another match when it comes from the match factory.[9]

Circa 1903

We must make the cars simple. I mean we must make them so that they are not too complicated from a mechanical standpoint, so that people can operate them easily, and with the fewer parts the better.[10]

Circa 1903

Any customer can have a car painted any color that he wants so long as it is black.[11]

Circa 1909. Ford limited production to black cars because black paint dried the fastest, speeding up production.

I will build a motor car for the great multitude. It will be large enough for a family but small enough for the individual to run and care for. It will be constructed of the best materials, by the best men to be hired, after the simplest designs the modern engineering can devise. But it will be so low in price that no man making a good salary will be unable to own one—and enjoy with his family the blessings of hours of pleasure in God's great open spaces.[12]

Circa 1909

We took what was a luxury and turned it into a necessity and without trick or subterfuge. When we began to make our present motor car the country had few good roads, gasoline was scarce, and the idea was firmly implanted in the public mind that an automobile was at the best a rich man's toy. Our only advantage was lack of precedent.[13]

No new models, no new motors, no new bodies and no new colors.[14]

Circa 1909, on the virtues of standardizing vehicles

I'm going to democratize the automobile. When I'm through everybody will be able to afford one and about everyone will have one. . . . [T]he automobile will be taken for granted.[15]

Circa 1909–10

I'm not worried about the market for automobiles. I'm not worried because some of my own backers think I'm crazy. They'll change their minds.[16]

Circa 1910

[Soon] automobiles will be going two abreast, in two directions on Woodward Avenue, and at the same time. And just as sure as that day is coming, so is coming a shorter workday, and so is a daily wage. It will be a daily wage of five dollars, perhaps as much as ten dollars, and maybe more. We are just beginning to get moving in the automobile industry.[17]

Circa 1913–20

In 10 years the motor driven vehicle has developed from a so-called freak to one of the most useful servants of men.[18]

February 16, 1913, *Boston Daily Globe*

There's no object in building it so only a few rich men can own one. It isn't the rich men who need it; it's the common folks like me.[19]

Circa 1917

The proper system, as I have in mind, is to get the car to the people.[20]

Circa 1917–20

Now, the Ford car is something more than a commodity. It is the first step in the demonstration of the practicability of the idea that it is possible for people to live well and comfortably without undue drudgery. The Ford car has made it possible for everyone to have means of transportation for himself and his family and his merchandise or farm products. It makes life in the country no longer a lonely, isolated existence.[21]

September 1918, *World's Work*

Every time I reduce the charge for our car by one dollar, I get a thousand new buyers.[22]

Circa 1918–22

[The automobile] has given the farmer a chance to get acquainted with the world, to see what is going on around him, to become a social being.[23]

November 1921, *Review of Reviews*

Well, gentlemen, so far as I can see the only trouble with the Ford car is that we can't make them fast enough.[24]

Circa 1922, response to Ford dealers who sought improvements to the Model T

The world is on wheels and will never get off.[25]

May 20, 1923, *New York Times*

[A]ll of my early partners said that the thing to do was to get out new models every year so that people would want to purchase the latest model just like women get a new hat each year. My hunch was that one model built to last a life time would go better and time has proven that I was right.[26]

Circa 1923

[Y]ou can dissect a Ford but you cannot kill it.[27]

Circa 1923. Ford vehicles were highly repairable.

It is my ambition to have every piece of machinery, or other non-consumable product that I turn out, so strong and well made that no one ought ever to have to buy a second one.[28]

Circa 1923

When one of my cars breaks down I know I am to blame.[29]

Circa 1923

There are no "remote" places in this country. The automobile has corrected that.[30]

January 1924, *Motor*

The demand for cars has not been satisfied. The need and the demand will be endless.[31]

August 10, 1924, *New York Times*

It isn't extravagance, a family needs an automobile.[32]

September 18, 1925, *New York Times*

[T]he automobile, by enabling people to get about quickly and easily, gives them a chance to find out what is going on in the world—which leads them to a larger life that requires more food, more and better goods, more books, more music, more of everything.[33]

October 1926, *World's Work*

We have remade this country with automobiles. But we do not have these automobiles because we are prosperous. We are prosperous because we have them.[34]

Circa 1926

The time is coming when an automobile will be so right that it will need no more service than a bar of soap.[35]

Circa 1926–27

Now, one of the first things that a man wants on the day he turns ambitious is a motor car. It typifies the new happiness that he is going to get for himself and his family.[36]

June 23, 1929, *New York Times*

The best thing I can do for the country is to create industry by building good motor cars.[37]

Circa May 1933, comment made in response to government and public pressure to contribute to Depression relief

Visitors often ask me what the car of the future will be. I don't know. If I did I would be making it now.[38]

February 1936, *American Magazine*

I've got no use for a motor that has more spark plugs than a cow has teats.[39]

Circa 1937–40, reaction to his son's automotive ideas

I fooled people with the Model A, and five years later I really made them sit up with the V-8. The experts said it couldn't be done. Cadillac had tried it in 1925, but it hadn't been a success. But I knew the eight-cylinder engine block would be better balanced, if we could just cast it in one piece.[40]

Circa 1942–44

[W]e've got to go back to the Model T days. We've got to build only one car. There won't be any Mercury, no Lincoln, no other cars.[41]

Circa 1942–44. Following the death of his son, Edsel, Ford reverted to past successes.

On Racing Automobiles

I never thought anything of racing, but the public refused to consider the automobile in any light other than a fast toy. Therefore . . . we had to race.[42]

Circa 1923

On the Model T

As we see it, Model T is the acme of motor car perfection.[43]
  Circa 1913

You can do that over my dead body.[44]
  Circa 1918, response to suggested changes to the Model T

We had to do it. But you know, the only thing wrong with the Model T was that people got tired of looking at it.[45]
  Circa 1919

There was no guessing as to whether or not it would be a successful model. It had to be.[46]
  Circa 1923

Maybe I should have done it sooner.[47]
  Circa 1927–30, on abandoning the Model T in 1927

The only thing wrong with that car was that people stopped buying it.[48]
  Circa 1927

Now, this is responsible for everything. This is the car that did the work. I do hope that everyone appreciates what it has meant to the world. It meant a *good bit*.[49]
  Date unknown

On the Model A

But this is a brand new car from the ground up. It was a long time coming, because we were determined that each part should be done right and thoroughly in the first place.[50]
  December 4, 1927, *New York Times*

The change [from the Model T] isn't revolutionary. It seems strange to me that we could put out such a car without employing one single new basic principle. We have simply done everything better than it was ever done before.[51]

January 7, 1928, *Literary Digest*

On Tractors

What this machine will do that is of world-wide importance is to keep young men on the farm.[52]

June 19, 1915, *New York Times*

The tractor is and always has been my pet hobby. It is something that will do much toward the betterment of mankind, and that is what I am largely interested in.[53]

March 13, 1918, *New York Times*

While all the rest of the plants are turning out destructive implements of war—necessary to force peace, it seems—this tractor plant is producing the one constructive weapon.[54]

April 6, 1918, *Literary Digest*

Of all the modern machines, the tractor is one of the greatest mechanical blessings that has been devised for humankind.[55]

July 1922, *Popular Science*

My first love was a farm implement, something that would take the burden off people and put it on steel and motor power. Now I have come back to my first love.[56]

Circa 1923

On Airplanes

I didn't take a flight to convert me to flying. I took a trip because Colonel Lindbergh asked me to; I couldn't help it.[57]

August 12, 1927, *New York Times*, reaction to his first flight with Charles Lindbergh

Aviation will not come into its own until the automobile has been absolutely perfected.[58]

June 1936, *Rotarian*

On Submarines

My idea of a submarine is a pill on a pole. That is, a pole on the front end of the submarine with a pill—bomb—on the end of it. The submarine—a small one, carrying one man—goes right up to the ship and sticks the pill against the hull. The submarine then withdraws and the torpedo goes off. That would settle the ship; and it can be done—what's to prevent it? [59]

February 10, 1917, *New York Times*

On Space Travel

I believe the time will come when man will even know what is going on in the other planets, perhaps be able to visit them.[60]

December 18, 1928, *New York Times*

2 ⚙ On the Ford Motor Company, Business, and Management

Automobiles were a risky investment in the 1890s, so it is not surprising that Henry Ford's first automotive corporation, the Detroit Automobile Company, founded in 1899, failed two years later. The Ford Motor Company, established in 1903, might have suffered a similar fate were it not for Ford's vision. Henry Ford parlayed his belief in high-quality, low-priced, mass-produced vehicles into reality. Sales skyrocketed, and Ford found himself at the head of a highly profitable corporation.

Central to Henry Ford's business philosophy was the concept of hard work. If there were issues between management and labor, they would be solved if both parties worked harder. Labor provided workers with the ability to support themselves and offered them redemption. Ford hired ex-convicts because he believed that "whether [a man] has been in Sing Sing or at Harvard . . . all he needs is the desire to work."[1]

While Henry Ford claimed to be a benevolent manager, historians would argue that his policies were more pragmatic. The five-dollar day was adopted because assembly-line work resulted in a 380 percent rate of employee turnover, not because of Ford's benevolence.[2] His standard response to employee grievances was to fire complainers, and his hatred of unions was legendary.

Montage showing Henry Ford, the Mack Avenue Building (*above*), River Rouge Plant (*below*), and Edsel Ford. Mack Avenue was the first Ford Motor Company factory and operated from approximately 1903 to 1905. Begun in 1917, Ford's River Rouge complex would eventually cover an area a half mile wide and a mile long, have ninety-three buildings, and employ as many as one hundred thousand workers at a time. From the Collections of the Henry Ford, THF23904.

Ford's auto plants and assembly lines were models of efficiency, but the management of the larger organization was not. He discouraged interoffice communication, making it difficult for different departments to work together. By refusing to assign job titles to management and executive staff, he made it all but impossible to establish accountability for management decisions. He did not value a college education and believed any man could do any job in his organization. Sometimes this resulted in a capable individual rising in the ranks, but often employees were assigned tasks beyond their capabilities. Though Henry Ford claimed to advocate limited supervisorial oversight, he often micromanaged employees.

On the Ford Motor Company

To do as much as possible for everybody concerned . . . [t]o make money and use it, give employment, and send out the car where people can use it . . . incidentally to make money.[3]

Circa 1916, on the purposes of the Ford Motor Company

We do not want any hard, man-killing work about the place, and there is now very little of it.[4]

Circa 1923

There is not much personal contact [between employees]—the men do their work and go home—a factory is not a drawing room.[5]

Circa 1923

We want to make men in this factory as well as automobiles.[6]

Circa 1923, referring to his revolutionary pay and benefits, which Ford believed would induce employees to better living

You see, this is my business. I built it and, as long as I live, I propose to run it the way I want it run.[7]

Circa 1923–24

The Sermon on the Mount is the covenant of our organization. We try to do unto others as we would have others do unto us.[8]

April 1924, *Good Housekeeping*

This business is a tool. If it is the largest tool of its kind, it should do the greatest work.[9]

July 1928, *American Magazine*

There is no business where chickens come home to roost more certainly than in the automobile business. The car has got to be good. And the only way it can be unquestioningly good is through good workmanship.[10]

Circa 1928–30

The American people have made the Ford Motor Company what it is. We have nothing the public did not give us.[11]

February 28, 1932, *New York Times*

[I]f we ever have to start selling stock in our company we will be wrecking our plant brick by brick. It would be the beginning of the end.[12]

December 2, 1932, *New York Times*

We pioneered on the eight-hour day, the five-day week, and the minimum wage that was higher than the market rate, but we did not do this because of regulation and compulsion. We did it because we were free to do what we thought was right.[13]

June 16, 1933, *New York Times*

I'm the general manager here and if I ever find out there's another general manager around here, I'll fire him.[14]

Circa 1933–45, reaction to a staff member who called himself the Ford Company general manager

You know gentlemen, in an organization as big as ours we must have an occasional son of a bitch.[15]

Circa 1933–45, referring to the employees who acted as a shield between Ford and the press and public

We'll probably change everything they do, anyway.[16]

Circa 1933–45, comment on departing a Ford Motor Company board meeting

On Business

Business is a service, not a bonanza.[17]

Circa 1916–19

Business is a process of give and take, live and let live.[18]

February 1919, *State Service: The New York State Magazine*

I have noticed that an efficient business organization is always built up around one man.[19]

Circa 1919, on his decision not to have stockholders in his tractor business

Business is never so good and sound and healthy as when, like a chicken, it must do a certain amount of scratching for what it gets.[20]

February 26, 1921, *Literary Digest*

If you can set the smallest business going, you have done something at which the biggest men often fail.[21]

Circa 1922

It is amazing how many men would like to regard industries as perennial Christmas trees which hang with free fruits. No industry has anything but what is put into it by the men who are in it.[22]

Circa 1922

Every business that employs more than one man is a partnership. This is so whether the man at the head of the business acknowledges it or not.[23]

Circa 1922

There is too much of the "my" and too little of "our," both in the shops and the head office. The workman has got to assume that it is "our" business. It is the only way he can feel that it is "his" business, too.[24]

Circa 1922

Business men go down with their businesses because they like the old way so well they cannot bring themselves to change.[25]
Circa 1923

I do not believe a man can ever leave his business. He ought to think of it by day and dream of it by night.[26]
Circa 1923

The public should always be wondering how it is possible to give so much for the money.[27]
Circa 1923, on the value and quality of Ford automobiles

Now a business, in my way of thinking, is not a machine. It is a collection of people who are brought together to do work and not to write letters to one another. It is not necessary for any one department to know what any other department is doing.[28]
Circa 1923. Ford deplored paperwork and interoffice communication.

It is not necessary to have meetings to establish good feeling between individuals or departments. It is not necessary for people to love each other in order to work together. Too much good fellowship may indeed be a very bad thing, for it may lead to one man trying to cover up the faults of another.[29]
Circa 1923

Paternalism has no place in industry.[30]
Circa 1923. After Ford's Sociological Department was closed in a 1920 reorganization, he distanced himself from its former policies.

Old-time business went on the doctrine that prices should always be kept up to the highest point at which people will buy. Really modern business has to take the opposite view.[31]
Circa 1923

If a business is not increasing, it is bound to be decreasing, and a decreasing business always needs a lot of financing.[32]

Circa 1923

It is one of nature's compensations to withdraw prosperity from the business which does not serve.[33]

Circa 1923

A great business is really too big to be human.[34]

Circa 1923. During the 1920s, Ford began to distance himself from his employees.

Some organizations use up so much energy and time maintaining a feeling of harmony that they have no force left to work for the object for which the organization was created. The organization is secondary to the object. The only harmonious organization is an organization in which all the members are bent on the one main purpose—not to get along with itself, but to get along toward the objective.[35]

Circa 1923

I pity the poor fellow who is so soft and flabby that he must always have "an atmosphere of good feeling" around him before he can work. . . . Not only are they business failures; they are character failures also; it is as if their bones never attained a sufficient degree of hardness to enable them to stand on their own feet.[36]

Circa 1923. Given Ford's criticism of, and behavior toward, his son, Edsel, he likely considered Edsel in this "weak" category.

In our business we prefer doers to talkers.[37]

October 31, 1924, *Boston Daily Globe*

The best place for a factory man's office is under his hat.[38]

January 1926, *System*

Big business is not money power: it is service power.[39]
Circa 1926

This is the country of big business. But . . . big business controls nothing. It is entirely at the mercy of public demand.[40]
Circa 1926

We do not have to ask for the public regulation of business. The public has always regulated business.[41]
Circa 1926

I'm cocksure about the future of American business.[42]
May 21, 1928, *Time*

No lamp posts have been provided for weak or overstimulated business to cling to and so they are apt to cling to one another. The embrace is called a merger.[43]
Circa 1928

If an employer does not share prosperity with those who make him prosperous, then pretty soon there will be no prosperity to share. That is why we think it is good business always to raise wages and never to lower them. We like to have plenty of customers.[44]
August 1929, *North American Review*

A market is never saturated with a good product, but it is very quickly saturated with a bad one.[45]
Circa 1930

A business ought not to drift. It ought to march ahead under leadership. The easy way is to follow the crowd and hope to make money. But that's not the way of sound business. The way is to provide a service. Try to run a business solely to make money and the business will die.[46]
Circa 1932

I have always felt that our first duty was to do the right thing, and that this would lead us to money sufficient to carry the right thing.[47]

February 1936, *American Magazine*

A business that makes nothing but money is a poor kind of business.[48]

Circa 1936

People often talk about business as if it was lower than other human activities. If a plant is producing something worthwhile, it's just as sacred as a home.[49]

Circa 1936

On Monopolies

Competition cannot be abolished; every attempted monopoly is an added impetus to a whole round of competition. Big business, so far from destroying competition, only raises up bigger competitors. The bigger the stride toward monopoly, the bigger the compensating competition.[50]

November 14, 1925, *Dearborn Independent*

Monopoly, like every other sort of absolute monarchy, creates a vacuum, which Nature is said to abhor.[51]

October 31, 1936, *Saturday Evening Post*

Monopoly means stagnation; stagnation means unemployment and mass unemployment means industrial, commercial and social decay.[52]

July 29, 1941, *New York Times*

On Management

In my factory every man shall keep his job as long as he wants it.[53]

Circa 1917. Despite Ford's intentions, the Ford Motor Company would have several large-scale layoffs while Henry Ford was at the helm.

In our plants, you do not see a lot of bosses standing around. The boss is largely superfluous. He creates class feeling. Work is delayed for his approval. He is likely to hold up actual performance. We manage to get along without him and do better than if we had him.[54]

December 4, 1921, *Boston Daily Globe*. Workers at Ford plants were evaluated by foremen as well as efficiency experts.

Jobs that are unnecessary to production are not jobs. They are cancers eating into the body of people's earnings. Cutting them out is curative.[55]

Circa 1922

Common sense in business administration appears to be so unusual that it is "news."[56]

Circa 1922

It is not the DRIVE of the boss that makes production; it is the loyal good-will of the workers.[57]

Circa 1922

You can drive a machine until it breaks—you must not drive men that way.[58]

Circa 1922

Welfare work that consists in prying into employees' private concerns is out of date.[59]

Circa 1922. Ford had recently closed his Sociological Department, which operated from 1913 to 1920 and investigated employees' living conditions and personal lives.

Foremen are only human. It is natural that they should be flattered by being made to believe that they hold the weal or woe of workmen in their hands. It is natural also that being open to flattery, their self-seeking subordinates should flatter them with still more to obtain and profit by their favor. That is why I want as little as possible of the personal element.[60]

Circa 1923

Propaganda, bulletins, lectures—they are nothing. It is the right act sincerely done that counts.[61]

Circa 1923

Management, unless its purpose be kept always in view, may degenerate into a thing of red tape which does not manage at all.[62]

January 16, 1926, *Literary Digest*

We do not have conferences, we do not have committees, we have no formal procedures of any kind. There is no formal method for interdepartment communications, because we do not have departments—if one man wants to say something to another man, he says it over the telephone.[63]

January 16, 1926, *Literary Digest*

The business of management is to manage. The thing to be managed is work.[64]

January 16, 1926, *Literary Digest*

Hiring two men to do the job of one is a crime against society.[65]

July 11, 1926, *New York Times*

When you fill a shop with fear, making men slaves who bend to their tasks when the overseer's eyes are upon them and slacken when the "boss" passes on—you haven't free industry at all. You are running a sort of prison.[66]

July 11, 1926, *New York Times*

The unfit employer causes more trouble than the unfit employee. You cannot fire the employer. He stays in control because he is the owner.[67]

Circa 1936

On Manufacturing

The most economical manufacturing of the future will be that in which the whole of the article is not made under one roof—unless, of course, it be a very simple article.[68]

Circa 1923

The place to start manufacturing is with the article. The factory, the organization, the selling, and the financial plans will all shape themselves to the article.[69]

Circa 1923

On Bureaucracy

That which one has to fight hardest against in bringing together a large number of people to do work is excess organization and consequent red tape. To my mind there is no bent of mind more dangerous than that which is sometimes described as the "genius for organization."[70]

Circa 1923

[W]e have no elaborate records of any kind, and consequently no red tape.[71]

Circa 1923

On Experts and Specialists

The expert is a good man to tell you what was being done down to closing time, day before yesterday.[72]

November 1921, *Review of Reviews*

If ever I wanted to kill opposition by unfair means I would endow the opposition with experts. They would have so much good advice that I could be sure they would do little work.[73]

Circa 1923

None of our men are "experts." . . . The moment one gets into the "expert" state of mind a great number of things become impossible.[74]

Circa 1923

On Safety

Accident prevention is an essential part of the industrial program. While we take great pleasure in giving employment to maimed men, we believe we are doing far greater work by preventing this maiming of men.[75]

Circa 1924

On Service

A manufacturer is not through with his customer when a sale is completed. He has then only started with his customer. . . . If the machine does not give service, then it is better for the manufacturer if he had never had an introduction, for he will have the worst of all advertisements—a dissatisfied customer.[76]

Circa 1923

It has been thought that business existed for profit. That is wrong. Business exists for service.[77]

Circa 1923

A business absolutely devoted to service will have only one worry about profits. They will be embarrassingly large.[78]

Circa 1932–42

On Quality

Quality is what counts, and nothing but quality.[79]

September 1918, *World's Work*

On Profit

And let me say right here, that I do not believe we should make such an awful profit on our cars. A reasonable profit is right, but not too much.[80]

Circa November 1916

We don't seem to be able to keep profits down.[81]

Circa November 1916

Without a profit, business cannot extend. There is nothing inherently wrong about making a profit. . . . It cannot be the basis—it must be the result of service.[82]

Circa 1923

If a man does a thing good, and does it the best he can, with the idea of service to other people, the profit will inundate him.[83]

May 16, 1926, *New York Times*

The money profits—the surplus you speak of—came from the people. We look upon them simply as a public trust which must be put back into the manufacture of something that will help men and women to better and more productive lives.[84]

July 31, 1928, *New York Times*

Profits are merely what we think we work for. . . . The real profit is not what the promoters get, but what the country gets.[85]

July 7, 1929, *New York Times*

On Consumerism

There are always enough people ready and anxious to buy, provided you supply what they want and at the proper price.[86]

Circa 1923

Purchasers really have to be trained and led as though they were an army.[87]

Circa 1924

Make things easy for the plain people to buy. That makes work. That makes wages. That makes surplus for extension and greater service.[88]

Circa 1926

It is because people never will become 100 per cent satisfied with everything they have that we never will reach the saturation point in anything that we produce.[89]

May 20, 1930, *New York Times*

On Advertising

A satisfied customer is our best advertisement.[90]

March 1917, *System*

Advertising? Absolutely necessary to introduce good, useful things; bad when it's used to create an unnatural demand for useless things, as it too often is.[91]

November 1921, *Review of Reviews*

No stunt and no advertising will sell an article for any length of time. Business is not a game.[92]

November 1921, *Review of Reviews*

Cut it all out. . . . I never did believe in it.[93]

August 9, 1926, *Time*. Ford banned advertising for several years.

I think we'll have good times if we don't do too much advertising. A good thing will sell itself. . . . We must make good things in this country, and not do too much talking about them. You've just got to let people know where to get them, and that's all.[94]

May 16, 1926, *New York Times*

Advertising should be used for education. . . . It should teach something, and simply tell the truth.[95]

Circa 1928

A car has got to sell itself.[96]

Circa 1928–32, response to being asked, "Do you think advertising sells a car?"

On Competition

Hurting the other fellow is bound to hurt me sooner or later.[97]

Circa 1917

No, destructive competition benefits no one. The kind of competition which results in the defeat of the many and the overlordship of the ruthless few must go. Destructive competition lacks the qualities out of which progress comes. Progress comes from a generous form of rivalry. Bad competition is personal.[98]

Circa 1923

To do one thing well stimulates others to do it better.[99]

Circa 1926

We have no desire to take business away from any automobile manufacturer. Our thought has always been that the automobile business is prosperous only when all the makers of good cars are busy.[100]

August 20, 1927, *Literary Digest*, response to competition between Ford Motor Company and General Motors Corporation

There should be rivalry between men. There should be rivalry between businesses.[101]

July 1928, *American Magazine*

Besides, there's no fun in a one-man race.[102]

July 1928, *American Magazine*

If a business be devoted to service it can have no competition.[103]

October 26, 1930, *New York Times*

Our competitors are behind all tax and N.R.A. [National Recovery Administration] plans, with the bankers' international and they are running all the governments of the world.[104]

Circa 1933, one of Ford's more paranoid statements

As far as competition is concerned, that must continue. But we must learn what competition really is. It is a striving to attain the best. To throttle it would mean to stop all progress.[105]

June 1936, *Rotarian*

3 ⚙ On Money and Economics

Henry Ford's views on money were contradictory. Though he was the nation's first billionaire, he claimed money was worthless. His Sociological Division penalized employees for insufficient savings, but he told young people to spend, not save, their money. He criticized the nation's gold standard but had a million dollars' worth of gold in a Detroit bank.

An advocate of laissez-faire economics, Ford believed the markets should be left to regulate themselves. He disdained politicians and economists who tried to tinker with the economy. Banks and bankers were beneath contempt for what he perceived as their attempts to control and limit the exchange of money. This hatred extended to Jews, who he believed controlled banking.[1]

After the turn of the twentieth century, the United States endured a number of booms and busts that finally culminated in the Great Depression. Millions of Americans lost their jobs, businesses, and homes. Though the Ford Motor Company was forced to limit production and lay off workers, Henry Ford refused to acknowledge the hard times, declaring, "I think these are the best times we ever had."

Henry Ford, January 1916. Courtesy of the Library of Congress, LC-USZ62-62286.

On Money and Finance

Money the Root of all Eval [*sic*].[2]
Date unknown, likely before 1917, from one of Ford's notebooks

Money has no value anyway. It is merely a transmitter, like electricity. I try to keep it moving as fast as I can, for the best interests of everybody concerned.[3]
Circa 1917

Money's only a lubricant to keep business going.[4]
Circa 1917

I would rather hear that a man made a million plows than that he made a million dollars.[5]
Circa January 1919

Money is but a tool.[6]
July 1928, *American Magazine*

Money, as such, has little to do with prosperity because in itself it does not produce.[7]
July 1928, *American Magazine*

If money is your only hope of independence, you will never have it.[8]

August 1929, *American Magazine*

More brains are being retarded by the striving for money than any other thing.[9]

February 24, 1930, *Time*

Money is like an arm or a leg—use it or lose it.[10]

November 8, 1931, *New York Times*

Money serves the same purpose in industry that wheels do in transportation. Both money and wheels are of value only if they can be used. Now, who would think of hoarding wheels and calling them wealth? Yet that is exactly what has been done with money.[11]

March 26, 1933, *New York Times*

You cannot eat a million dollars.[12]

July 1933, *Good Housekeeping*

We must get rid of the idea of making money out of money. Money is not a commodity. A million dollars in gold by itself will not produce one copper penny. Put a hen on it and it will not hatch. Water it and it will not grow.[13]

Circa 1933

I have never known money to be a sufficient motive for any useful achievement. The achievement comes first; the money afterward.[14]

August 1942, *Rotarian*

Thinking about money interferes with one's efficiency. If a man is doing work worth while, it requires all his brain power.[15]

April 8, 1947, *Toledo (Ohio) Blade*

On His Own Money

I have more money now than I can use, and I feel I am simply custodian of what I have. It was intrusted [*sic*] to me by the people.[16]
January 3, 1916, *Boston Daily Globe*

Whatever it is, the less money I have the less trouble I have.[17]
July 24, 1919, *New York Times*

I do not care any more for money than a housewife cares for coal for her kitchen range. It keeps the kettle boiling. Money as money, money as a private fortune, means nothing to me.[18]
May 9, 1923, *Outlook*

Money means nothing to me. There is nothing I want that I cannot have. But I do not want the things money can buy.[19]
May 19, 1923, *Time*

We'll have to wait for my secretary. I haven't any money.[20]
June 4, 1934, *Time*, on trying to purchase a history pamphlet at Gettysburg

Oh Shit![21]
Date unknown, reaction to being told he was the first American billionaire

On Saving Money

Frankly, I do not believe in bank accounts for boys because they so often give boys a wrong idea as to how to get ahead. It is all very nice to save up for a rainy day when you grow up, but there is no reason why boys should wrap their foundations around their bank accounts.[22]
January 25, 1919, *New York Times*

People who ultimately come by real money never do it by saving.[23]
November 1921, *Review of Reviews*

There's nothing in saving money. The thing to do with it is to put it back into yourself, into your work, into the thing that is important, into whatever you are so much interested in that it is more important to you than money.[24]

November 1921, *Review of Reviews*

On Debt

It is inevitable that any one who can borrow freely to cover errors of management will borrow rather than correct the errors.[25]

Circa 1923

The rock on which business breaks is debt.[26]

Circa 1932

The lower the debt the better the business, and that goes for government.[27]

May 9, 1938, *Time*

On Economics

The market will take care of itself.[28]

Date unknown

A subsidy means getting something from the Government for nothing.[29]

January 15, 1922, *New York Times*

Overproduction! It's a false word. When you say a thing has been overproduced, all you can possibly mean is that it is wrong in price or wrong in time.[30]

Circa 1927

No great business ability is needed in finance.[31]

November 14, 1925, *Dearborn Independent*

The trouble with economists is that they read more than they think.[32]

May 24, 1931, *New York Times*

The economic system is not to be found in books, but in actual affairs. Many of the book theories have been scrapped, whether the economists know it or not.[33]

May 24, 1931, *New York Times*

We are going to remodel our economic machinery so that it will not fly to pieces when it gets out on the road. It is a pretty good system—when it works.[34]

November 8, 1931, *New York Times*

Scarcity breeds speculation, and speculation is only a word covering the making of money out of the manipulation of prices, instead of out of supplying goods and services.[35]

February 1, 1936, *Saturday Evening Post*

On Banks and Bankers

I believe the whole world would benefit tremendously if all interest on money were abolished.[36]

October 29, 1922, *New York Times*

Bankers play too great a part in the conduct of industry. Most business men will privately admit that fact. They will seldom publicly admit it because they are afraid of their bankers.[37]

Circa 1923

The average successful banker is by no means so intelligent and resourceful a man as is the average successful business man. Yet the banker through his control of credit practically controls the average business man.[38]

Circa 1923

When bankers get into a business they usually destroy it.[39]

February 1, 1933, *New York Times*

The first duty of a bank is to be a safe repository for money. . . . It's just as if I put my car in a garage and when I came to get it, I found somebody else had borrowed it and run it into a tree.[40]

March 6, 1933, *Time*

I have had dealings with lawyers but never with bankers.[41]

July 25, 1943, *New York Times*

On Wall Street

I would tear down my plants, brick by brick, with my own hands, before I would let Wall Street get ahold of them.[42]

Circa 1915–20. Another source from the same interview reports that Ford said "Jew speculators," not "Wall Street."

Wall Street is progressive and possibly indispensable. It buys when something is ready for junking. It doesn't finance the business of twenty-five years hence. It takes the dying success, squeezes out the last drop and tosses it away. That's why I say Wall Street is progressive. It disposes of the antiquated and obsolete.[43]

October 19, 1924, *New York Times*

On the Stock Market

It is just more or less respectable graft.[44]

Circa 1923

The only stock I take any stock in is stock in the stock room.[45]

June 20, 1926, *New York Times*

I don't know anything about the stockmarket.[46]

February 24, 1930, *Time*

It doesn't really matter whether the stock market goes up or down.[47]

May 29, 1930, *New York Times*

Everyone has been looking for Santa Claus. When the stock market rises a few points, a great number of people become very happy, for they think Santa Claus has come. But when the prices go down, so also do their spirits, for they then begin to fear that perhaps there is no Santa Claus. When everyone becomes convinced that there is no Santa Claus we shall be on a sound basis.[48]

May 16, 1931, *Saturday Evening Post*

There is not a great deal of difference between the mental attitude of the man who stands in a bread line and that of the man who sits around watching the prices of stocks. Both are out for the same thing.[49]

May 16, 1931, *Saturday Evening Post*

On the Gold Standard

To dig some kind of metal out of the ground and make that the measure of the world's wealth and buying power seems to me a ridiculous proposition. The brokers of the country can't see that, of course, for they are parasites thriving on the present system, and they will continue it as long as they can. You can't argue with a parasite.[50]

June 20, 1926, *New York Times*

Gold is the most useless thing in the world.[51]

August 4, 1928, *Milwaukee Sentinel*

On Prosperity and Wealth

I believe it is better for the nation, and far better for humanity, that between 20,000 and 30,000 people should be contented and well fed than that a few millionaires should be made.[52]

January 11, 1914, *New York Times*

For me, it was when Mrs. Ford stopped cooking.[53]

Circa 1915, on the greatest hardships of wealth

Wealth wouldn't be such a curse if everybody helped carry it.[54]

August 26, 1922, *Collier's*

Wealth does not change men. The possession of it does not spoil them, as is so often claimed. Wealth simply reveals what there is in a man. It lifts the lid and gives what is in him a chance to come out. If the bad stuff comes to the surface, it is because it was there and was only waiting for a chance to express itself.[55]

Circa 1923

Prosperity cannot exist without a confidence in what the future may hold.[56]

June 1928, *World's Work*

On Greed

Greed is merely a species of nearsightedness.[57]

Circa 1923

On Depressions and the Great Depression

Oh, that's all right. I can use all the unemployed making tractors.[58]

Circa 1917, responding to the prospect of a depression following World War I

We need to keep up the people's spirit and you cannot do that with talk; you must do it by action. One expenditure made in faith in the future is worth all the words any can say.[59]

May 29, 1930, *New York Times*, spurring people to make purchases

It's a good thing the recovery is prolonged. Otherwise the people wouldn't profit by the illness.[60]

Circa 1930–35

This "depression" we hear about is due to laziness! People wanted something for nothing. . . . They wanted to gamble on the stock exchange. They didn't want to work. The crash was a good thing; it has made them start working and thinking again.[61]

October 13, 1930, *Time*

Dishonesty caused the so-called depression. People inflate stocks —that's dishonest. People buy inflated stocks with the hope of getting rich at the expense of someone else. That's also dishonest. Persons of that type are too gullible. They cannot understand. They need experience.[62]

March 15, 1931, *Fort Myers (Fla.) Press*

The depression is a wholesome thing in general.[63]

October 21, 1931, *New York Times*

Stop looking backward for the times that are dead, and do not look toward your government for anything more than government.[64]

July 31, 1932, *New York Times*

There is no Santa Claus in times like these. No one to pull us out, so we must stop waiting for something to happen and get busy.[65]

August 28, 1932, *New York Times*

If you lost your money, don't let it bother you. Charge it up to experience.[66]

Circa 1932–39

There is nothing wrong with the world. I think these are the best times we ever had.[67]

February 1, 1933, *New York Times*

A great thing has occurred among us. We have made a complete turn around and at last America's face is to the future. Three years—1929 to 1932—we Americans looked backward. All our old financial and political machinery was geared to pull us out of the depression by the same door through which we entered. . . . It failed. We now realize that the way is forward—through it. Thanks for that belongs to President Roosevelt. Inauguration day he turned the Ship of State around.[68]

Circa April 1933. Despite his words, Ford had little respect for Roosevelt.

Simple human honesty, without greedy over-reaching, would lift us out of our troubles in a week.[69]

June 16, 1933, *New York Times*

Everybody is going to survive this period. Nobody is going to starve.[70]

July 1933, *Good Housekeeping*

Why, the depression would be over for the whole country very soon if American industrialists would just forget these alphabet schemes and take hold of their industries and run them with good, sound American business sense.[71]

November 10, 1934, *Newsweek*. "Alphabet schemes" refer to government recovery programs known by acronyms like NRA for the National Recovery Act.

4 ⚙ On Employees and Ford's Social Policies

According to the media and his own biographers, Henry Ford's labor policies were revolutionary. He pioneered profit sharing, the five-dollar day, the five-day week, and the eight-hour day. His schools educated employees, and his hospital treated them at a reasonable cost. He also hired African Americans, former prison inmates, and the handicapped at a time when others would not.

The reality of working in Ford factories was often different from Ford's stated aim to reward hard work. The five-dollar day, as noted in chapter 2, was created to keep employees from fleeing assembly lines. It worked. Production tripled, and labor time was slashed by 88 percent.[1]

Very few employees actually made that five-dollar wage. Efficiency experts established impossible standards and quotas. Even employees who ate lunch at their machines, took no time for breaks, toileting, or sharpening tools, couldn't achieve it.[2] The average salary was $2.34 per day.[3] When automobile sales and profits fell, Ford's solution of lowering automobile prices forced an additional speed-up. As one Ford executive described it: "We were driving them in those days. . . . Ford was the worst shop for driving men."[4]

In addition, to be eligible for higher wages and profit sharing, employees had to conform to certain moral standards. Ford's "Sociological Department" worked to ensure that employees didn't smoke, drink, gamble, house boarders, or act immorally. Standards were relaxed when the department closed in 1920.

In March 1932, when the Depression forced Ford to lay off fifty thousand to sixty thousand workers, a Communist group organized a "Ford Hunger March." The protesters were tear-gassed and sprayed with freezing water; one man was fatally shot. When the marchers still continued to advance, a submachine gun killed four men and wounded nineteen.[5]

Workers on a Ford Motor Company assembly line. Courtesy of the Library of Congress, LC-USZ62-44478.

Henry Ford had no tolerance for unions because he believed they sought to limit productivity and control workers. He barred union activity and assigned the former boxer Harry Bennett to intimidate labor organizers and members. In May 1937, Ford employees attacked United Auto Workers members distributing pamphlets near the Ford River Rouge plant. Reporters and photographers who witnessed the orchestrated attack called it the "Battle of the Overpass." The images and stories, which appeared in newspapers all over the world, were a discredit to Ford and helped fuel union activity. In 1941, a sit-down strike by the United Auto Workers closed the River Rouge plant. When Ford resolved to break up the company rather than negotiate with the union, his wife stepped in. Fearing there would be no company left for their son and grandchildren, Clara threatened to leave Ford if he did not sign an agreement. Ford complied and signed an agreement, which in the end was better than both General Motors and Chrysler contracts at the time.

On Employees

Nobody is ever discharged here unless he becomes quite a hopeless case. No, we just take hold of him. We've always done that.[6]

April 1914, *Everybody's Magazine*

Well, there are only two things to make a man unhappy here. One is that he hasn't enough work to do, and the other is that he has trouble at home. We can give him more work in the shop. That is easy.[7]

April 1914, *Everybody's Magazine*

You can trust your employees every time if you give them half a chance. . . . I have been a workman myself, and I know.[8]

Circa 1915–17

My ambition is to employ still more men; to spread the benefits of this industrial system to the greatest possible number, to help them build up their lives and their homes. To do this, we are putting the greatest share of our profits back into the business.[9]

Circa 1916

Every man who works for me is going to get enough for a comfortable living. If an able-bodied man can't earn that, he's either lazy or ignorant. If he's lazy, he's sick. We'll have a hospital. If he's ignorant, he wants to learn. We'll have a school. Meantime, figure out in the accounting bureau a scale of profit-sharing that will make every man's earnings at least five dollars a day.[10]

Circa 1917

There ought not be employers and workmen—just workmen. They're two parts of the same machine. It's absurd to have a machine in which one part tries to foil another.[11]

Circa 1917

Men don't work for money alone. . . . Above all, he must have something to hope for in the future.[12]

May 4, 1918, *Literary Digest*

Old employees, like old friends, are best.[13]

Circa 1922

The undirected worker spends more of his time walking about for materials and tools than he does in working; he gets small pay because pedestrianism is not a highly paid line.[14]

Circa 1923

[T]he average workman is more interested in a steady job than he is in advancement. . . . But the vast majority of men want to stay put. They want to be led. They want to have everything done for them and to have no responsibility.[15]

Circa 1923

[T]he difficulty is not to discover men to advance, but men who are willing to be advanced.[16]

Circa 1923

None of the men work too hard.[17]

Circa 1923

My men are my partners.[18]

Circa 1923

Idle men and machinery produce nothing but disorder and misery.[19]

August 20, 1924, *Boston Daily Globe*

One's own employees ought to be one's own best customers.[20]

Circa 1926

Workmen go out of doors, go on picnics, have time to see their children and play with them. They have time to see more, do more—and incidentally, they buy more. This stimulates business and *increases prosperity*, and in the general economic circle the money passes through industry again and back into the workman's pocket. It is a truism that what benefits one is bound to benefit all.[21]

Circa 1928

On African Americans as Employees

We have several thousand [African Americans] in our plant, and no trouble.[22]

November 14, 1923, *New Republic*

On Prison Labor and Parolees as Employees

I will take your discharged inmates as fast as they come out, and put them to work.[23]

September 9, 1915, *New York Times*

Only three out of six hundred convicts in my factory have failed to make good.[24]

Circa 1915–20

On the Handicapped as Employees

The blind man or cripple can, in the particular place to which he is assigned, perform . . . just as much work and receive exactly the same pay as a wholly able-bodied man. We do not prefer cripples—but we have demonstrated that they can earn full wages.[25]

Circa 1923

I wouldn't keep those blind men a minute if I did not believe them efficient.[26]

Circa 1923

There are no outcasts with us. We never turn a man down because of physical deformities, or taint of any kind providing his disease is not contagious.[27]

Circa 1923

We have jobs for blind men and jobs for one-legged men—in fact, a job for nearly any kind of a man. And more than this, we want crippled men about and we want blind men about—if for no other reason than in order to assure the others that physical disability does not mean the poor house.[28]

December 1926, *World's Work*

On Wages

If you expect to get anything out of a man nowadays you must pay him well. If you want the best there is in him, you must make it really worth his while. You must give him something to live for.[29]

January 11, 1914, *New York Times*

But in a partnership of skilled management and honest labor, it is the workman who makes high wages possible.[30]

October 1922, *Current Opinion*

Paying good wages is not charity at all—it is the best kind of business.[31]

Circa 1922

The man who contributes much should take away much.[32]

Circa 1923

The payment of five dollars a day for an eight-hour day was one of the finest cost-cutting moves we ever made.[33]

Circa 1923

You cannot get good work out of poorly paid men.[34]

April 7, 1930, *New York Times*

Wages are the only thing that should be high in this country.[35]

May 24, 1931, *New York Times*

Half-paid men do not increase the consumption of goods. Workmen who receive only part of their proper wages are unable to buy houses or radios or automobiles or education for their children.[36]

May 24, 1931, *New York Times*

The hardest thing I ever did was to reduce wages.[37]

Circa 1933–34

The only formula for providing prosperity is, through the aid of science, to produce the largest possible amount of goods with the least possible amount of human labor, marking each lowering of the cost of production by an increase in wages and a decrease in selling price. If this principle be carried out through distribution and service, real wages will continually rise and the amount of goods called for will employ every human being who needs employment. And sufficient wealth in usable things will be created to supply all needs.[38]

February 1, 1936, *Saturday Evening Post*

On Profit Sharing

All our men have helped us in our business. We feel they are entitled to share in the profits.[39]

January 11, 1914, *New York Times*

On the Five-Dollar Day

We believe in making 20,000 prosperous instead of a few slave-drivers rich.[40]

Circa January 1914

As for this plan of mine, it has nothing to do with any "ism" whatever. Our company is making money enough to do some good in the world and I'm glad to do it.[41]

Circa 1914–17. Some called Ford's policies socialism.

But when we established a minimum wage of $5 a day for workers in the Ford plant my business acquaintances said I was crazy, the profiteers called me an anarchist, and my kind friends prophesied my speedy bankruptcy. Well, we have made and sold more cars and better cars and sold them at the lower price since I began to pay the higher wages than we did before.[42]

September 1918, *World's Work*

Some people thought I took a big risk when I started paying that high wage. But I felt the money the company was making wasn't mine. It was meant to be shared with those who created it. That's sound philosophy.[43]

Circa 1932

On the Five-Day Week

Every man needs more than one day a week for rest and recreation.[44]

May 5, 1922, *Akron Weekly Pioneer Press*

People need an extra day of rest so they can be fit to enjoy Sunday. I think it would be good for business, too. If the people are tired out on Saturday, or if they are worrying, they cannot buy from merchants. The whole market might be helped if a five-day week were practiced.[45]

August 10, 1924, *New York Times*

The five-day week, by giving people the sixth day for physical recreation and the seventh for religious observance, will go far toward bringing Christianity nearer to the people.[46]

November 13, 1926, *Dearborn Independent*

A six-day week is all right for machines but a five-day week is enough for men.[47]

January 14, 1929, *Time*

On Ford's Sociological Department

We now have forty-five investigators, who are interviewing all of the employees. Every detail of their living is inquired into. Our investigators do much more than take their names and addresses. We inquire and learn the nationality, the religion, the bank savings, whether the man owns or is buying property, how he amuses himself, the district he selects to live in—this and much else are tabulated.[48]

April 19, 1914, *New York Times*

It is our business to see that they spend their money right. That applies not only to the men out there in the shop but to every one in this organization, all the way up to the top. We have stopped some of our highest paid men from spending money improperly.[49]

April 1914, *Everybody's Magazine*

We had to have [the Sociological Department] first in order to be able to see that the men made proper use of their profits. We know there are some out there who can't stand prosperity.[50]

April 1914, *Everybody's Magazine*

On the Eight-Hour Day

Any one big enough to look over and beyond the rim of a round silver dollar can see that an eight-hour day is not only better for the men but better for the employer as well.[51]

September 3, 1916, *New York Times*

The eight-hour day has meant an increase in the efficiency and the loyalty and the self-respect of every one on the payroll. I am in favor of the passage of a Federal law that will make eight hours the national working day.[52]

October 7, 1916, *New York Times*

As a matter of fact, I don't believe in any hours for work. A man ought to work as long as he wants to, and he ought to enjoy his work so much that he wants to work as long as he can. It's only monotonous, grinding work that needs an eight-hour day. When a man is creating something, working to get results, twelve or fourteen hours a day doesn't hurt him.[53]

Circa 1917

On Unemployment

Lack of employment ought to be as rare in the United States as snow in the tropics.[54]

Circa 1922

Any shut-downs should be right in the middle of Summer. The Summer is the time for vacations in the United States. Then the people can put up a tent in a corner and live or go touring in their car.[55]

July 30, 1930, *New York Times*

Unemployment is not a natural phenomenon, but the visible result of ignorance of economic health laws.[56]

August 10, 1930, *New York Times*

[What Unemployment insurance] really does is to insure that we shall always have unemployment. . . . But unemployment which means anxiety and destitution is both unnatural and unnecessary. We do not want to insure it; we want to abolish it.[57]

May 16, 1931, *Saturday Evening Post*

Unemployment is not solely an employer's problem; it is society's problem.[58]

May 24, 1931, *New York Times*

The word "unemployment" has become one of the most dreadful words in the language.[59]

June 13, 1932, *Time*

On Labor and Unions

It is a matter on which we congratulate ourselves that we have never had a particle of trouble with labor unions. They have never succeeded in organizing our factory. We pay better than anybody else, and we keep close to our men. I keep going through the shops all the time.[60]

January 11, 1914, *New York Times*

We don't know such a thing as a union labor man in this plant, but we recognize human beings and their right to just wages.[61]

May 24, 1916, *Boston Daily Globe*

[A] strike is only the voice of the God of Greed calling for more profit.[62]

September 3, 1916, *New York Times*

War between capital and labor is just like any other kind of war. It happens because people do not understand each other.[63]

Circa 1917

There can be no settlement of these strikes so long as the moneyed interests of Wall Street continue in their efforts to dominate American industry. They are behind these walkouts, as they are behind every disturbance in the ranks of labor or capital. Get them out and you will succeed in bringing industrial peace.[64]

August 10, 1922, *New York Times*

We don't either encourage or discourage unions.[65]

November 1921, *Review of Reviews*

That's the great tragedy of American labor today, these simple, honest men believe they have been organized for their own good by their own kind of men.[66]

September 14, 1922, *New York Times*

The men probably don't know it, and maybe their leaders don't even know that they are really but tools in the hands of the master exploiters of . . . human productive energy.[67]

Circa 1924

That goes for labor unions, too; they are all organized and used by Wall Street.[68]

October 31, 1925, *New York Times*

You know it is the capitalists who organize the workingmen; they don't organize themselves.[69]

May 11, 1926, *Boston Daily Globe*

As far as I am concerned, labor unions do not exist. The worker can be what he pleases, Catholic, Lutheran, Jew or trade unionist. But we don't allow any of those things to be discussed during working hours. We pay what we consider right and organized labor is not represented in my factories.[70]

Circa October 1930

Labor unions are the forerunners of Communism.[71]

Circa October 1930

Bigness and the unions have broken up the closeness there was between boss and worker. . . . Even without the unions it's hard to have personal contact with the men any more. The plants have grown so big.[72]

Circa 1932

This is not a strike—it's an attack on the Ford industries.[73]

January 29, 1933, *New York Times*, on the Briggs plant strike

The actual truth is that certain bankers are trying to obtain control of the Ford concern. Certain of my competitors are operating against me, supported by these bankers, with the object of preventing another Ford car from leaving the factory.[74]

February 6, 1933, *Time*, response to picketers at the Briggs Plant in Detroit

I have never sought to prevent our men from joining any association—religious, racial, political or social. No one who believes in American freedom would do that. When our men ask about unions, I give them the same advice as when they ask of the other schemes that are always being aimed at men's wages. I say to them: "First, figure out for yourself what you are going to get out of it. If you go into a union, they have got you, but what have you got?"

We think our men ought to consider whether it is necessary for them to pay some outsider every month for the privilege of working at Ford's. Or, whether the union can do more for them than we are doing.[75]

April 14, 1937, *New York Times*

There shouldn't be any bargaining or dealing necessary between employers and employe[e]s. Our company pays the best wages it can and always has. . . . We're all workers together, the men and I.[76]

April 19, 1937, *Time*

What was the result of these strikes? Merely that numbers of men put their necks into an iron collar. We're only trying to show who owns the collar.[77]

May 24, 1937, *Time*, from a Ford Company brochure designed to discourage unionism

Labor union organizations are the worst thing that ever struck the earth because they take away a man's independence.[78]

Circa 1937

It is just one of those things that help fasten control upon the necks of labor.[79]

Circa 1937. The Wagner Act, also called the National Labor Relations Act, limited businesses' ability to control union activities.

Financiers are behind the unions and their object is to kill competition so as to reduce the income of the workers and eventually bring on war.[80]

Circa 1937

I want a strong, aggressive man who can take care of himself in an argument, and I've got him.[81]

Circa 1937, on his controversial decision to name Harry Bennett as his representative to conduct union negotiations

A union is like a big spider's web. Once inside the web the workman can't move.[82]

March 9, 1941, *New York Times*

All men want is to be told what to do and get paid for doing it.[83]

March 17, 1941, *Time*

I'm not going to sign that contract! As far as I'm concerned the key is in the door. I'm going to throw it away. I don't want any more of this business. Close the plant if necessary. Let the union take over if it wishes.[84]

Circa May 1941, on his refusal to sign the United Automobile Workers contract

Labor unions are here to stay. We of the Ford Motor Company have no desire to "break the unions," to turn back the clock.[85]

Circa June 1941, a conciliatory Ford after signing the UAW contract

5 ⚙ On Work
and Leisure

Henry Ford fervently believed in the redemptive value of work. He reasoned that work not only supported individuals, but wages also provided them with a sense of self-worth. He simply could not imagine how anyone could be happy without work.

Because of this strong work ethic, as a young man Ford considered leisure and recreation a waste of time. That changed when his Model T caused him to see the economic value of leisure. In his own words, "People must have leisure to consume what they produce."

Ford was ahead of his time in his views on exercise. He was famous for jogging and challenging others to foot races and chin-up contests decades before regular exercise was advocated for adults. His interest in exercise spurred a movement to revive old-fashioned dances, including square dancing.

On Work

No one can fight and honestly work at the same time. No one can manipulate stocks and honestly work at the same time. If everyone works hard and honestly there can be no hard times.[1]

April 11, 1915, *New York Times*

Henry Ford chopping wood during a 1921 camping trip. Ford was fond of a quote credited to Henry David Thoreau: "Wood warms you twice, once when you chop it and again when you burn it." Courtesy of the Library of Congress, LC-F8-15234.

Instead of sending soldiers down to Mexico we should send industrial experts down there—missionaries of the true and holy gospel of Get Down to Work.[2]

April 11, 1915, *New York Times*

A normal, healthy man wants to work.[3]

Circa 1917

[T]he day's work is a great thing—a very great thing. It is at the very foundation of our economic place in the world; it is the basis of our self-respect; it is the only way to reach out and touch the whole world of activity.[4]

Circa February 1919

All of us are workingmen these days. If we are not, we are parasites. No amount of money excuses any man from working. He is either producer or parasite—take your choice.[5]
Circa February 1919

Who is so pitiable as the man without an occupation?[6]
Circa February 1919

If he intends to remain always a manual labourer, then [a man] should forget his work when the whistle blows, but if he intends to go forward and do anything, the whistle is only a signal to start thinking over the day's work in order to discover how it might be done better.[7]
Circa 1923

Idle hands and minds were never intended for any one of us. Work is our sanity, our self-respect, our salvation. So far from being a curse, work is the greatest blessing. It is only when it is mixed with indolence or injustice that it becomes a curse.[8]
Circa 1923

Blindfold me and lead me down there into the street and let me lay my hands by chance on the most shiftless and worthless fellow in the crowd and I'll bring him in here, give him a job with a wage that offers him some hope for the future, some prospects of living a decent, comfortable and self-respecting life, and I'll guarantee that I'll make a man out of him.[9]
Circa 1923

My gospel is work. If a man is down and out the only thing that will save him is work—work that will give him something to live on and live for.[10]
Circa 1923

I used to enjoy my work because I was always thinking how I could do my work better. It is the spirit of good workmanship that makes work a joy.[11]

Circa 1923

One reason the world has moved forward so slowly is because the people have been deadened with too much work.[12]

Circa 1923

More than anything else people want the chance to work. It does no good to carry them on your back.[13]

August 10, 1924, *New York Times*

I don't believe anybody ever died from overwork.[14]

May 11, 1926, *Boston Daily Globe*

Work does more than get us our living; it gets us our life.[15]

Circa 1926

The trouble with the world is too much brain work without the normalizing balance of hand work.[16]

June 1927, *Atlantic Monthly*

Nothing is particularly hard if you subdivide it into small jobs.[17]

October 1, 1927, *New York Times*

I am not working merely for today or only for myself. I believe that we should do all we can, not only for ourselves but also for posterity. Otherwise our achievements would hardly be worth while.[18]

November 21, 1927, *New York Times*

Most great work is done in quiet.[19]

Circa 1928

Work done without an intelligent understanding of its underlying principles becomes meaningless. It makes a mere machine of the worker.[20]

August 4, 1929, *Milwaukee Sentinel*

[W]ork is the remedy for all things.[21]

March 7, 1930, *New York Times*

When all is said and done, the ability to work means more than anything else.[22]

October 1930, *Harper's Magazine*

Everyone is capable of doing at least twice as much as he or she is now doing.[23]

Circa 1930

The average man, however, won't really do a day's work unless he is caught and cannot get out of it. There's plenty of work to do if people would do it.[24]

March 15, 1931, *Fort Myers (Fla.) Press*

There is no way for the people of this country to live without work. There is no way for the people of the world to live without work. And the sooner the world is rid of the notion that there may be a way, the better off we shall be.[25]

May 16, 1931, *Saturday Evening Post*

[T]here is only one thing in the world that makes prosperity, and that is work.[26]

July 26, 1931, *New York Times*

Work? Work? Is there anything to do but work?[27]

May 29, 1932, *New York Times*

Our greatest possession is the right to work. That is not a right which someone can guarantee to us. It is a right which we must guarantee ourselves.[28]

February 1, 1936, *Saturday Evening Post*

A man's job is his best mental health insurance. A man wrapped up in his work is protected from worry.[29]

February 1936, *American Magazine*

Nothing is hard to do unless you think it is.[30]

Circa September 21, 1938

The unhappiest man on earth is the one who has nothing to do.[31]

September 1944, *Rotarian*

On Retirement

I shall never retire. I shall be in business as long as I live.[32]

Circa 1923

Men should not retire. I haven't retired. The thing to do is to keep on working.[33]

September 18, 1925, *New York Times*

The man who retires doesn't get much happiness.[34]

May 11, 1926, *Boston Daily Globe*

I shall never give up business so long as I feel that I am of service to humanity.[35]

May 9, 1928, *New York Times*

Oh, it would be easy to quit. I could take a few thousand dollars and live comfortably for the rest of my life, in fact live just as well as I live now.[36]

July 1928, *American Magazine*

On the Assembly Line and Repetitive Labor

I could not possibly do the same thing day in and day out.[37]
Circa 1922

I have not been able to discover that repetitive labour injures a man in any way.[38]
Circa 1923

Repetitive labor—the doing of one thing over and over again and always the same way—is a terrifying prospect to a certain kind of mind. It is terrifying to me. I could not possibly do the same thing day in and day out. But, to other minds, perhaps I might say to the majority of minds, repetitive operations hold no terrors. In fact, to some types of minds, thought is absolutely appalling.[39]
Circa 1923

Study the way you are doing things! See how many steps in any particular process you can eliminate. An inefficient process is almost invariably a "dirty" one. All waste is a kind of dirt.[40]
August 1929, *American Magazine*

On Leisure and Recreation

What's the value of recreation, anyhow? It's just a waste of time. I got my fun out of my work.[41]
Circa 1917

In my mind nothing is more abhorrent than a life of ease. None of us has any right to ease. There is no place in civilization for the idler.[42]
Circa 1923

Every man who works ought to have sufficient leisure. The man who works hard should have his easy chair, his comfortable fireside, his pleasant surroundings. These are his by right. But no one deserves ease until after his work is done.[43]

Circa 1923

People must have leisure to consume what they produce.[44]

May 16, 1926 *New York Times*

What is really bothering most people is how to put in their spare time. That used to bother only what was called the "leisure class."[45]

Circa 1926

I think young people could get a great deal of recreation out of their work.[46]

Circa 1928

I do nothing because it gives me pleasure.[47]

March 17, 1941, *Time*

On Exercise

Energy should be spent on something useful. Children ought to learn to swim in case a boat tips over. They ought to play games so they'll be strong enough to protect themselves.[48]

Circa 1925–30

When my system needs toning up I like to go out into the woods and alternately walk and run. By running I don't mean just a jog or a dog-trot, but a good brisk clip which thoroughly "warms up the engine."[49]

October 1934, *American Magazine*

Exercise is bunk. If you are healthy you don't need it. If you are sick you shouldn't take it.[50]

Circa 1930–40

On Ice Skating

People who enjoy skating are often down-to-earth people.[51]

Circa 1932–38, comment made after falling on the ice

On Dance

The dance is one of the oldest forms of human expression. Some have regarded it as a part of human speech. From the dance of atoms, through the mating dance of certain birds and animals, up to the tribal dances of the various nations, the expression of emotion and ideas in rhythmic movements of the body bears all the indications of a deep natural instinct.[52]

August 15, 1925, *Literary Digest*

Square dances to me are beautiful for the same reason that a Colonial interior is beautiful. It is the tradition behind them. I like the formal movements, the studied steps, the graceful figures. There is nothing haphazard about them. You either know them or you do not. They bring back a time that was less hurried and more neighborly.[53]

August 16, 1925, *New York Times*

I find the modern dances formless and unattractive in every way. That's why I want to revive the old.[54]

August 16, 1925, *New York Times*

Manners and dance go together. The formal dance, the leisurely dance, requires formal manners and more polished manners. I am old-fashioned enough to like good manners.[55]

August 16, 1925, *New York Times*

The old American dancing was clean and healthful. . . . The old dances were social. The modern dances are not.[56]

Circa 1928–30

6 ⚙ On Machines and Technology

To Henry Ford, the machine was "the new messiah," and technology's promise was limitless. He scoffed at the idea that new machines would reduce the number of jobs. Machines freed humanity from backbreaking work. "The Man minus the machine is a slave. Man plus the machine is a free man," he reasoned.

New technology enabled people to truly connect with one another by automobile travel, through radio, airplanes, and other inventions. He believed the resulting globalism would "soon bring the whole world to a complete understanding."[1]

Despite his admiration for Thomas Edison and other inventors, Ford did not believe there was such a thing as an original invention. Innovation was instead the inevitable product of progress.

On Machines and the Machine Age

Modern industrial development hasn't changed a single rule of life—and cannot![2]

Circa 1922

I think that unless we know more about machines and their use, unless we better understand the mechanical portion of life, we cannot have the time to enjoy the trees, and the birds, and the flowers, and the green fields.[3]

Circa 1923

Henry Ford with a steam engine, July 22, 1944. Courtesy of Wayne State University Virtual Motor City Collection, Ford, Henry; Agriculture (2491).

Power and machinery, money and goods, are useful only as they set us free to live. They are but means to an end.[4]

Circa 1923

Machines are to a mechanic what books are to a writer. He gets ideas from them, and if he has any brains he will apply those ideas.[5]

Circa 1923

A machine that has been used for 25 years is always more interesting than a new one; it has a story to tell, and shows where its weaknesses were.[6]

May 11, 1926, *Boston Daily Globe*

The effect of labor-saving devices is not to diminish the number of men employed but to increase it.[7]

October 11, 1926, *New York Times*

The Machine is the new messiah.[8]

Circa 1927–29

Machinery is accomplishing in the world what man has failed to do by preaching, propaganda, or the written word.[9]

Circa 1928

Real prosperity depends on machinery. To those who say this will produce idleness, the reply is it's just the other way. It will produce work. For making machines means making more machines, and consequently you have more production and better wages.[10]

April 11, 1928, *New York Times*

Machines were devised, not to do a man out of a job, but to take the heavy labor from man's back and place it upon the broad shoulders of the machine.[11]

May 29, 1930, *New York Times*

The world is coming to a point where machines will do the greatest part of creative labor, but because of this men will not be thrown into idleness.[12]

March 17, 1931, *New York Times*

The machine is the best servant man has ever had and will perform still greater tasks for him, making life more comfortable, refined and humane, more worth the living.[13]

March 17, 1931, *New York Times*

This talk about the machine mastering man is book talk. Man will always master the machine, because he made it.[14]

May 24, 1931, *New York Times*

The machine age is barely started now. In the real machine age which is to come the dirt and ugliness and confusion and noise and disregard of human rights which are all about us today will be done away with.[15]

May 24, 1931, *New York Times*

It is nonsense to call the machine a Frankenstein monster which is crushing its creator. The machines are not driving men out of work. Quite the contrary. . . . Machines must be built by other machines, and it takes men to build them and other highly paid men to design them.[16]

February 1, 1933, *New York Times*

There will never be a technocracy in the sense of a ruling mechanical oligarchy, because life will not stand for it.[17]

February 1, 1933, *New York Times*

Machines without men are useless. All real power is the power within man; power in a machine is the power of man extended. Machines do not run themselves. It takes a high intelligence to run them. . . . Without that intelligence directing them they would be idle. Indeed, the danger is that men's intelligence will lag behind the machines which he creates.[18]

June 1936, *Rotarian*

Man minus the machine is a slave. Man plus the machine is a free man.[19]

Circa 1936–40

On Planned Obsolescence

It is considered good manufacturing practice, and not bad ethics, occasionally to change designs so that old models will become obsolete and new ones will have to be bought . . . because repair parts for the old cannot be had. . . . We have been told this is good business, that is clever business. . . . Our principle is precisely to the contrary. . . . We want to construct some kind of a machine that will last forever.[20]

Circa 1923

On Inventions and Inventing

To teach that a comparatively few men are responsible for the greatest forward steps of mankind is the worst sort of nonsense.[21]

Circa 1920–29

An invention or device that is useful is always a matter of evolution. On the "Model T" car, of which we have built 5,500,000, was one device which I patented, and was sure nobody could get. Afterward I found that the same thing precisely had been patented in 1826 by a piano tuner![22]

January 1922, *Current Opinion*

In truth, there are no exclusive discoveries. Nothing is ever entrusted to one man alone.[23]

Circa 1928

New inventions come along when the old ones are beginning to arrive at a stage of perfection.[24]

June 1936, *Rotarian*

We have just touched the fringe of our inventive genius.[25]

August 1942, *Rotarian*

7 ⚙ On Politics and Government

Less government was better government, according to Henry Ford. He viewed politicians, political parties, and government employees as ineffective at best, downright destructive at worst.

Politics held so little interest that Ford seldom voted. Because of his business success, many suggested he run for political office. He ignored them until 1918, when President Woodrow Wilson urged him to run for the vacant Michigan seat in the U.S. Senate. Ford had never served in public office, had no experience in government, and had little knowledge of civics. He made no campaign speeches, raised no funds, and refused to make any political appearances. Despite these shortcomings, he nearly won.

Even before Ford ran for the U.S. Senate, he was urged to vie for president. "Ford for President" clubs sprang up throughout the nation, and influential people like Will Rogers endorsed him.[1] Though Ford flirted with a presidential run, he never officially declared his candidacy.

"YES, WE HAVE NO AMBITIONS TODAY!"

This Clifford Berryman cartoon parodies Henry Ford's presidential aspirations—or lack thereof. The title references the popular 1923 song "Yes, We Have No Bananas!" Courtesy of the U.S. Senate Collection, Center for Legislative Archives, National Archives.

On Politics

Even in the United States we let those whom we have elected to office be swerved from their duty. We do not assert ourselves.[2]

January 3, 1916, *New York Times*

You know, I really know nothing about politics.[3]

October 7, 1916, *New York Times*

All this campaign spending is bunk. I wouldn't give a dollar to any campaign committee.[4]
Circa 1916

I could find a man in five minutes who could tell me all about it.[5]
Circa July 1919, in response to a question about his familiarity with civics

I could read it if I wanted to know.[6]
July 17, 1919, *New York Tribune*, when asked about the Declaration of Independence

Governments get things done because they have the power to command power, they have unlimited means to ride over all mistakes.[7]
Circa 1922

Our help does not come from Washington, but from ourselves.[8]
Circa 1923

The Government is a servant and never should be anything but a servant.[9]
Circa 1923

Governments can promise something for nothing but they cannot deliver.[10]
Circa 1923

It's too hard to find the Government, and you can't do business with people you don't know and can't find.[11]
October 19, 1924, *New York Times*

What the world chiefly needs to-day is fewer diplomats and politicians, and more men advancing from kerchiefs to collars.[12]
Circa 1926

The real business of the country is not at Washington, but everywhere, in every town and hamlet, in every family in the land.[13]
September 8, 1928, *New York Times*

Let the government stick to the strict function of governing. That's a big enough job. Let them let business alone. What is everybody's business is nobody's business.[14]

March 15, 1931, *Fort Myers (Fla.) Press*

Political measures to cure economic diseases always come after the crisis of illness has passed.[15]

May 16, 1931, *Saturday Evening Post*

If I were the government, instead of raising taxes at this time, I'd abolish them for a while, let people see the value of government and how much of it they are willing to pay for.[16]

May 29, 1932, *New York Times*

The power that makes the country is the people, not the Government.[17]

July 1933, *Good Housekeeping*

Government is a collective job which we delegate to others. It is not the be-all and end-all of American life.[18]

February 1, 1936, *Saturday Evening Post*

The trouble with government and finance is that our servants have set up as our masters, and they have not proved to be very wise masters.[19]

February 1, 1936, *Saturday Evening Post*

The trouble with the Presidency is that a man may say and intend one thing, but pressure may compel him to do something different.[20]

October 26, 1936, *Time*

If finance would get out of government and government would get out of business, everything would go again.[21]

May 9, 1938, *Newsweek*

On Political Parties

I'm a Republican, but I'm for Wilson. I'm a Republican for the same reason I have ears—I was born that way.[22]

September 28, 1916, *New York Times*

They will have to show me a difference before I affiliate with either party. They are both tarred with the same brush.[23]

Circa 1923

Political parties are of no importance. I don't believe in holding a party responsible.[24]

February 12, 1924, *Boston Daily Globe*

On Patriotism

The people of the United States are patriotic. But it is time for all to realize that patriotism does not consist merely of dying for one's country. I believe that patriotism consists more in living for the benefit of the whole world, of giving others a chance to live for themselves, their country and the world. A man is naturally patriotic, and to cry patriotism at him as is now being done throughout the country is more of an insult than a compliment.[25]

March 2, 1916, *Toledo (Ohio) Blade*

I think nations are silly and flags are silly, too. If the country is rotten, then the flag is rotten, and nobody ought to respect it. Flags are rallying points, that's all. The munitions-makers and the militarists and the crooked politicians use flags to get people excited when they want to fool them. I'm going to keep the American flag flying on my plant until the war is over, and then I'm going to pull it down for good; and I'm going to hoist in its place the Flag of All Nations, which is being designed in my office right now.[26]

November 1916, *Current Opinion*. Ford later claimed that the reporter "trapped me into saying things, put words in my mouth."[27]

On Nationalism

I do not believe in the kind of nationalism that tries to set one country up against another. That is what causes wars. It keeps people from understanding each other.[28]

September 1918, *World's Work*

On Voting

But so far as neglecting government is concerned, I am one of the worst offenders. I have been a voter for thirty-one years, and during that time I have voted but six times. Then it was because Mrs. Ford drove me to it.[29]

January 3, 1916, *New York Times*

Years ago, when I was just past my twenty-first birthday my father said to me: "Henry, you are a man now and a citizen, and it is time for you to vote." He took me to the voting place and advised me to vote for James A. Garfield for president. I did so.[30]

June 23, 1918, *New York Times*. Ford was twenty-one during the election of 1884, three years after Garfield's assassination.

I haven't voted for 20 years, but I am going to vote this time.[31]

November 9, 1936, *Time*

On Taxes

No one seems to care how much government costs, provided the money is raised from the other fellow.[32]

February 25, 1924, *New York Times*

From a purely selfish standpoint, it does not make the least difference to me whether the Government taxes me 1 per cent or 99 per cent. I do not know exactly, but I imagine I could live just as I now live on 1 per cent of my income.[33]

February 25, 1924, *New York Times*

High taxes on the rich do not take burdens off the poor. They put burdens on the poor.[34]

February 25, 1924, *New York Times*

On Tariffs and Free Trade

If we cannot compete on even terms with any country on earth then we ought to quit.[35]

September 28, 1916, *New York Times*

I cannot help thinking that tariff protection is an excuse of laziness.[36]

October 18, 1930, *New York Times*

On Socialism, Bolshevism, and Communism

I am not sure that I really know anything about socialism. . . . I don't believe socialism appeals to me; nor, I might say, do I regard our profit-distribution scheme as socialistic.[37]

January 11, 1914, *New York Times*

Bolshevism is now crying for the brains and experience which it yesterday treated so ruthlessly.[38]

Circa 1923

The various Socialistic programmes are nothing more than attempts to set up a public bookkeeper to keep everybody's accounts and determine everybody's share. They go somewhat farther and attempt to promise a life in which work will be only an incident.[39]

August 1929, *North American Review*

Socialism is the determination of the have-nots to take away the property of the haves.[40]

Circa 1936–40

On the National Recovery Act (NRA)

I was always under the impression that to manage a business properly you ought to know something about it.[41]

Circa 1933, response to increased government regulation of business during the Roosevelt administration

On a Senatorial Bid

I know nothing about parties' or party machinery, and I am not at all concerned about which ticket I am nominated on. They can put my name on all the tickets if they want to.[42]

September 1918, *World's Work*

If I can do some things for the good of all the people better in Washington than I can here, then I am willing to go to Washington for that reason—that and the President's request.[43]

September 1918, *World's Work*

If they want to elect me let them do so, but I won't make a penny's investment.[44]

Circa 1918

I would pitch a penny to decide which nomination I would accept, or leave it to my secretary to decide.[45]

Circa 1918

I have been commanded to run for Senator. And now—well, we shall see whether I can build anything but automobiles, tractors and ships.[46]

Circa 1918

This is where our danger lies; that is what makes for Bolshevism.[47]

November 16, 1918, *New York Times*, response to his senatorial loss, which he attributed to bolshevism and "manipulation by the moneyed interests"

[I] would not give five cents to be a United States Senator.[48]
  Circa 1918, upon losing the election

On a Presidential Bid

I don't want anything to do with it.[49]
  Circa 1914

Let them go ahead with it and see what happens. We might have some fun with these politicians.[50]
  Circa 1914, on being named for the Iowa primaries

I have no political aspiration of any kind whatever.[51]
  February 7, 1914, *New York Times*

I do not want anything to do with politics or political offices. The filing of my name at Lansing was a joke.[52]
  March 2, 1916, *New York Times*, on being listed as a Republican candidate for president

I'd just like to be down there about six weeks and throw some monkey wrenches into the machinery.[53]
  Circa 1916–18

I would not walk across the street to be elected President of the United States.[54]
  September 1918, *World's Work*

There is the kind of man I would appoint Secretary of the Navy.[55]
  Circa January 1922, regarding an unnamed business executive touring his plant

An interviewer asked me about my presidential ambitions. Said I: "I wouldn't step as far as from here to that rug to become King of England!"[56]
  May 28, 1923, *Time*

I am not a candidate for anything. I can't imagine myself today accepting any nomination. Of course, I cannot say, and no intelligent man can say, what I will do tomorrow. There might be a war, or some crisis of a sort, in which legalism and constitutionalism and all that wouldn't figure, and the nation wanted some person who could do things and do them quick.[57]

August 1, 1923, *New York Times*

That's where I'll be some day![58]

November 14, 1923, *New Republic,* referring to the White House

8 ⚙ On War
and Peace

Born in the last year of the Civil War, Henry Ford understood the long-term devastation resulting from armed conflict. When the nation was poised on the brink of World War I, he chartered a ship, the *Oscar II*, determined to sail to Europe and to stop it. By the time the ship arrived in Stockholm in January 1916, divisions and politics among the activists overwhelmed him. He decided to "go home to mother," meaning his wife, Clara.

Though Ford opposed both World War I and II, patriotism compelled him to supply vehicles and armaments for both conflicts. This decision bothered his conscience for the rest of his life.

On War

If there had been work enough there would have been no war.[1]
Circa January 1915

To my mind, the trouble with the nations of the earth is that they spend less money in getting ready to help people than they spend in getting ready to kill people.[2]
April 11, 1915, *New York Times*

Why do vast masses of mankind allow themselves to be marched off to the slaughter when in their hearts they know that when they die it will be in no good cause, but will be merely to satisfy the ambition of some greedy individual?[3]
April 11, 1915, *New York Times*

Henry Ford setting sail on the Peace Ship, *Oscar II*, at the pier in Hoboken, New Jersey, December 1915. Ford's well-intentioned but naïve attempt to stop war ended when, on arrival in Sweden, he decided to return to the United States. From the Collections of the Henry Ford, THF24051.

The saddest thing about this war—about every war, in fact—is that the people acquiesce to it. The moment we can get people not to acquiesce in war, to refuse to go to war, there will be no more war. Only the rulers will be left to fight. Such contests would be little prize fights between kings.[4]

April 11, 1915, *New York Times*

If war came here and I were offered treble prices to manufacture motor cars for military purposes I would burn down my plant before I would accept an order.[5]

April 11, 1915, *New York Times*. Ford would later produce materials during both world wars.

We hang, execute by electricity, or imprison for life those who counsel and abet retail murder; we decorate with crosses and stars, we honor and raise monuments to those who counsel and abet wholesale murder—we make millionaires of them.[6]

April 11, 1915, *New York Times*

The cause of militarism is never patriotism; it is usually commercialism.[7]

April 11, 1915, *New York Times*

New York wants war, but the United States doesn't. The peoples west of New York are too sensible for war.[8]

Circa June 18, 1915

The isolation of the United States is a perfect safeguard against invasion.[9]

August 23, 1915, *New York Times*

The writers of military treatises showing how Ja[p]an, or Germany, or any other nation could invade the United States under the guise of history and "military probabilities" are trying to fill the minds of the people with fear by the use of their high-sounding nonsense—that is what the whole thing is—nonsense.[10]

August 23, 1915, *New York Times*

I hate war, because war is murder, desolation and destruction, causeless, unjustifiable, cruel and heartless to those of the human race who do not want it, the countless millions, the workers. I hate it none the less for its waste, its uselessness, and the barriers it raises against progress.[11]

Circa August 22, 1915

The best thing that could happen would be for the nations of Europe to go bankrupt. They would be compelled to stop fighting.[12]

September 19, 1915, *New York Times*

Do you want to know the cause of war? It is capitalism, greed, the dirty hunger for dollars.[13]

November 15, 1915, *New York Times*

Out of the trenches by Christmas, never to return![14]

Circa November 24, 1915. His original exhortation, "We'll get the boys in the trenches home by Christmas," changed after a reporter explained that even if he could stop the war, it would be impossible to transport all the soldiers home by Christmas.

Every mother in the world should bring pressure to stop the war. It must be stopped in this country, for preparedness is war. No boy ever killed a bird without a slingshot or a club.[15]

November 25, 1915, *New York Times*

The biggest heroes and the greatest martyrs are the men lying out there in the trenches. Ask them what they are dying for—and I have asked men just from the trenches—and they will tell you they do not know.[16]

Circa December 1915

I'd give all of my money—and my life—to stop it.[17]

Circa 1915

No man ever armed himself even with a knife and fork unless he intended to attack something, if only an oyster or a piece of meat.[18]

January 3, 1916, *New York Times*

Before going to Europe I held the view that the bankers, militarists, and munition [*sic*] manufacturers were responsible. I come back with the firm belief that the people most to blame are the ones who are getting slaughtered. . . . They don't write enough letters to them and let them know their views.[19]

January 3, 1916, *New York Times*

There have been fine words about "preparedness" and "militarism" being totally different, but Europe knows today that the only difference is in the spelling.[20]

March 2, 1916, *Toledo (Ohio) Blade*

War is murder. I was a murderer. I was a helper of murder. When the crisis came we all took a hand. But it is all the same. War is murder.[21]

Circa 1916, on his company's war efforts

An army or navy is a tool for the protection of misguided, inefficient, destructive Wall Street.[22]

January 17, 1917, telegram

I never said I would not fight. I never said I would not do all for the country that I was able to do. I am a pacifist, but I want to say to you that a pacifist is the hardest fighter you ever saw when he finally is crowded into taking arms.[23]

February 6, 1917, *New York Times*

War is the most hideous waste in the world.[24]

Circa 1917

The common people, the people who lose most by fighting, don't know what they are fighting for. They fight because they are told to.[25]

Circa 1917

The way to end war permanently is to give everyone in the world a chance to get what he wants at a price he can afford to pay.[26]

September 1918, *World's Work*

I believe this will be the last war.[27]

September 1918, *World's Work*

They were fools to go on there. They were warned.[28]

July 24, 1919, *New York Times*, response to the sinking of the *Lusitania* in 1915

Just gold, that is the one and only reason for wars.[29]

December 4, 1921, *New York Times*

War is an orgy of money, just as it is an orgy of blood.[30]

Circa 1922

This is about all that guns are good for—to ornament a museum.[31]

Circa 1923

The world does not seem to be tired of war, in spite of the fact that everybody lost and nobody won in the last war.[32]

July 21, 1924, *New York Times*

Education's the way to stop wars.[33]

May 16, 1926, *New York Times*

Back in the war days the preachers were telling us that the United States and the world in general would get something worth while out of the war—something worth the sacrifice of human life. Well—did we get it? The war financiers got theirs. What did the rest of the world get?[34]

February 5, 1927, *New York Times*

I don't think there's any chance of war on any large scale. The last one was too much of an educator.[35]

April 11, 1928, *New York Times*

You can't end war by taking away the weapon that is at hand. Men fought before there were battleships or before there were guns.[36]

February 24, 1930, *Time*

Well, we made a plan to kill people and see who we killed![37]

Circa September 1931, on the death of Ford test pilot S. Leroy Manning

Through wars and dictatorship whole nations have ceased to be free.[38]

February 1, 1936, *Saturday Evening Post*

They don't dare have a war and they know it. It's all a big bluff. I don't know Hitler personally, but at least Germany keeps its people at work.[39]

September 11, 1939, *Time*

This so-called war is nothing but about 25 people and propaganda. Get them and you'll have the whole thing.[40]

October 2, 1939, *Time*

If Britain needs money, I favor giving them all they want. It will end the war in a hurry.[41]

December 16, 1940, *Life*

These planes will never be used for fighting. Before you can build them the war will be over.[42]

Circa 1941, on building B-24 Liberator bombers

We might as well quit making cars now.[43]

February 9, 1942, *Time*, comment made at the time of the bombing of Pearl Harbor, the previous December

I do believe that this war may be the last great war.[44]

August 1942, *Rotarian*

The reason we have war is that the world is not yet civilized.[45]

August 1942, *Rotarian*

Hunger has caused more wars, perhaps, than greed.[46]

August 1942, *Rotarian*

My message to young people, those in uniform and those out of uniform, is simply this: find out the cause of war. That will stop wars quicker than anything I know. I could tell them, but it doesn't seem to work that way, somehow. They must find out for themselves.[47]

Circa March 1944

We have progressed so rapidly in developing machinery for killing people that humanity could not survive another war.[48]

September 1944, *Rotarian*

On Peace

I'm for peace, first, last, and at all times, but not until it brings about the right conditions. And so I'm going to help fight for it. I'm at the Government's call.[49]

March 13, 1918, *New York Times*

Peace is a matter of education and Americans are too well educated to participate in another war.[50]

February 20, 1929, *Fort Myers (Fla.) Press*

I want peace, and I will fight like the devil to get it.[51]

April 8, 1947, *Toledo (Ohio) Blade*

On the Peace Ship

I'll give you a million dollars if you'll come.[52]

Circa December 1915, Ford's alleged offer to Thomas Edison to join the Peace Ship. Edison pretended not to hear him.

This crowd suits me exactly. It's just like a community. In a community we have old folks and young folks, rich and poor, men and women and children. Some people are more prominent, others less. Some have more ability than others. Our ship is just like that. It's just as though I had scooped up an average American community and transferred it to a ship.[53]

Circa December 1915. The various delegates, from pacifists to feminists, were described by the press as a "ship of fools" and "nuts."[54]

I consider that the peace ship will have been worth while if it does nothing more than it has done already in driving preparedness off the front page of the newspapers and putting peace on the front page.[55]

Circa December 1915

[I] had better go home to mother. . . . I told [Mrs. Ford] I'll be back soon. You've got this thing started now and can get along without me.[56]

Circa late December 1915. Ford left the Peace Ship early.

Peace has been given publicity.[57]

December 30, 1915, *Toledo (Ohio) Blade*

Many believed I had quit trying to establish peace. I purposely allowed that impression to prevail just to see what those advocates of preparedness would do.[58]

February 7, 1916, *New York Times*

I would send another peace ship or spend a million dollars in any other way if I thought that by doing so I could shorten the war a single day.[59]

September 1918, *World's Work*

I have no regrets and no apologies to make. I wanted to see peace. I at least tried to bring it about. Most men did not even try.[60]

Circa 1918

On Soldiers

To my mind, the word "murderer" should be embroidered in red letters across the breast of every soldier.[61]

April 11, 1915, *New York Times*. Ford later denied making the statement.

You don't compel a man to learn the candymaker's trade unless he wants to be a confectioner; why should you make him learn the soldier's trade if he doesn't want to be a butcher?[62]

April 11, 1915, *New York Times*

If I had my way, I'd throw every ounce of gunpowder into the sea and strip soldiers of their insignia.[63]

Circa April 1916

We would be sorry to see any of our men resign or enlist in the National Guard, but both recruits and State Militiamen will be treated alike—as though they quit the plant to engage in other lines of business.[64]

June 1916 announcement that soldiers would lose their jobs. Ford later denied making the statement.

I don't blame any man for avoiding military service.[65]

July 23, 1919, *New York Times*

We are giving and will give the servicemen [returning from war] preference in all jobs. . . . We want to help rehabilitate them and give them a new chance. . . . We can't do enough for these fellows.[66]

September 1944, *Rotarian*

On the Military

It would be splendid if we could enlist an army of men to make the desert bloom and make every mile of our streams and every foot of our land productive. That would be an Army of the United States indeed![67]

Circa 1922

Turn the Volstead Act enforcement over to the army and navy. They haven't anything to do in peace time, anyhow.[68]

June 10, 1923, *New York Times*, urging the armed forces to enforce prohibition

On Profiteering

I could today make vast sums from warfare if I so chose, but it would be better to die a pauper than that anything I have helped to make, or that any thought, word, or act of mine should be used for the furtherance of this slaughter.[69]

August 23, 1915, *New York Times*

Personally I am not going to touch a dollar of war profits. My share will be carried back into the United States Treasury.[70]

September 1918, *World's Work*. There is no record of Ford returning war profits.

I don't want any of it. It's like taking blood money. You can tell anybody and everybody that I am going to return it all.[71]

Circa 1918

9 ⚙ On Law, the Legal System, Crime and Punishment

Lawsuits were commonplace for Henry Ford and his company. George B. Selden, an early automobile patent holder, sued him for patent infringement in 1903. Ford prevailed when the courts declared Selden's patent invalid. In 1919, Ford sued the *Chicago Tribune* for libel after the newspaper called him an "ignorant idealist." He prevailed again, but was awarded a judgment of only six cents. In December 1927, Aaron Sapiro, a San Francisco lawyer, filed a defamation suit as a result of anti-Semitic articles in Ford's *Dearborn Independent*. After it became clear that he would likely lose the trial, Ford made a written apology and the lawsuit was dropped.

For someone with such pronounced ideas on personal responsibility, Henry Ford could be surprisingly forgiving. He employed hundreds of former convicts and felt a sense of responsibility for their rehabilitation. In the case of adultery, Ford had a more personal reason to urge leniency. The year he advised women to forgive their philandering husbands in the *Ladies' Home Journal* coincides with the birth of a boy who was likely his illegitimate son by Evangeline Dahlinger.

Portrait of Henry Ford, December 24, 1934. Courtesy of the Library of Congress, LC-USZ62-78374.

On the Law, Lawyers, and Lawsuits

Why do you want to be a lawyer, anyway? They're parasites.[1]
Circa 1916

You are a good enough attorney, I think, to get me to say this or that which would not be in my mind.[2]
July 19, 1919, *New York Times*, referring to the *Chicago Tribune*'s lawyer

Laws can do very little. Law never does anything constructive.[3]
Circa 1923

Laws do not save a country. Life changes too fast for that. By the time a law gets on the books, the situation it was designed to meet has altered. Laws cannot ruin a country.[4]
October 1934, *American Magazine*

We live in a big glass house here—we can't throw rocks.[5]
Circa 1935–45, on his reluctance to enter into lawsuits

And, above all else, keep away from lawyers. They are bound to get you into trouble.[6]

July 25, 1943, *New York Times*

On Justice and the Judiciary

All that is the matter with this world is injustice. Establish justice and everything will be all right.[7]

August 25, 1923, *Literary Digest*

Increase the salaries of the Supreme Court judges.[8]

August 25, 1923, *Literary Digest*, Ford's answer to the question of how to end injustice

On Patents

I believe absolutely in free competition, and in abolishing patents, which kill competition.[9]

November 1921, *Review of Reviews*

On Crime and Criminals

I have never met a man yet who was thoroughly bad. Every man has his good qualities and they will assert themselves if there is a chance. My experience with men is that they never get into trouble when they are kept busy. It is idleness that breeds crime.[10]

September 9, 1915, *New York Times*

And even if the young people are the folks who commit crime, they had the war to show them how to kill people, didn't they?[11]

May 16, 1926, *New York Times*

We are very efficient in seeing to it that a young man who is convicted never has a chance to go straight after he comes out of jail.[12]

December 1926, *World's Work*

The reason we have so much crime and racketeering is because schools do not teach our young men how to fit into the world.[13]

March 1, 1930, *Literary Digest*

On Adultery

The homes need not be wrecked if the wives or husbands who are innocent sufferers have an understanding of what life is. What are we on earth for? To get experience.[14]

September 1923, *Ladies' Home Journal*

I say to the woman whose husband is in this situation: Treat it like the measles! It's a disease that strikes lots of people. That's all it is, at the most. Help your husband through it. Stand by. Don't let it hurt you. Don't let it break up your home.[15]

September 1923, *Ladies' Home Journal*

How could something which made better men out of them really hurt their wives? It could hurt their vanity. It could hurt their pride. But these are the spirit of evil in us.[16]

September 1923, *Ladies' Home Journal*

Women! Why Hicks, women don't do you any harm. You can screw any woman on earth, excepting for one thing; never let your wife find out.[17]

Date unknown

On Capital Punishment and the Death Penalty

But we kill—or want to kill—the criminal, because it seems to be the easiest way of disposing of the problem. We are taking hold of both problems with the wrong handle. I wouldn't mind giving a man a licking, but I wouldn't want to kill him and I don't see how one can vote for capital punishment unless he, himself, were willing to be the executioner.[18]

February 5, 1927, *New York Times*

I am sure capital punishment is not a deterrent to crime. Any man who has reached the point of being willing to kill another does not care whether he himself gets killed.[19]

February 5, 1927, *New York Times*

It is wrong to kill a man. It does no good for the man and it does no good for society.[20]

Circa February 1927

I believe Sacco and Vanzetti should not be executed. If there is any doubt about the fairness of their trial, they should have a new trial. But in any event they should not be killed.[21]

August 10, 1927, *New York Times*, regarding two Italian immigrants who were convicted of murder. Vanzetti wrote to thank Henry Ford prior to his execution.

On Wills and Inheritance

I do not agree with the generally accepted principle that it is the duty of the parent to make financial provision for his offspring. . . . I hold that making such a provision is usually hurtful to the offspring rather than helpful.[22]

December 4, 1921, *Boston Daily Globe*

It would be said that people had bought these stocks for financial protection of their families, their children. Protection from what? From the necessity of earning their living? Their children would be better off if they had to finance themselves.[23]

March 11, 1922, *New York Times*

10 ⚙ On Education and the Arts

Though he praised McGuffey Readers and the works of Longfellow, Ford wasn't much of a booklover. At the 1919 *Chicago Tribune* trial, Ford repeatedly refused to read aloud for the court. Many were left wondering if Henry Ford was able to read at all.

His writing skills were limited. Though numerous books and newspaper and magazine articles are credited to the automaker, his coauthors and ghostwriters deserve most of the credit. As John Kenneth Galbraith noted, "His syntax and spelling have many of the rough-and-ready qualities of the planetary transmission."[1]

Ford held divergent views on art and music. Though he enjoyed the technical merits of the works of the painter Diego Rivera, he generally considered art wasteful and decadent. He found music pleasurable, especially the songs of Stephen Foster and square-dance pieces. Jazz, on the other hand, he believed to be degenerate.

On Education

I would like to get all the college professors in the world, bar none, and put them out in that factory, and then see what they would do with it.[2]

May 29, 1915, *Harper's Weekly*

Henry Ford receiving an honorary degree from the University of Michigan. Courtesy of Bentley Historical Library, University of Michigan, BL000146.

Education? Come to Detroit and I'll show you the biggest school in the world.[3]

Circa 1917, referring to his factories

To my mind, the usefulness of school ends when it has taught a man to read and write and figure.[4]

Circa 1917

I would not give a plugged nickel for all the higher education and all the art in the world.[5]

Circa 1917

I should say that the purpose of education is to make people do what they don't want to do. . . . They'll do what they want to do without being educated.[6]

Circa 1919

The hardest thing of all is to educate people. Most of them don't really want to learn and apply themselves.[7]

November 1921, *Review of Reviews*

The great trouble with the school experience is that the course is so long that the graduates are generally too old to go to work.[8]

March 1922, *Banker's Magazine*

A man may be very learned and very useless. And then again, a man may be unlearned and very useful. The object of education is not to fill a man's mind with facts; it is to teach him how to use his mind in thinking.[9]

Circa 1923

The successful teacher is one who can make a child want to go to school.[10]

August 16, 1925, *New York Times*

I believe the greatest thing there is is education.[11]

March 5, 1927, *Literary Digest*

The only way to really learn is by doing.[12]

June 1927, *Atlantic Monthly*

The trouble with much so-called modern education is that it ignores the physical basis of life. We are training children to inhabit a paper world. We teach them to assume that ink is preferable to action.[13]

June 1927, *Atlantic Monthly*

No one will ever get anywhere in this world unless he becomes a teacher, one who can show others how to do things.[14]

December 14, 1928, *New York Times*

The bigger education is gained through the discipline of life.[15]

Circa 1928

If taught properly every boy upon leaving school could go to an employer and say he was specifically fitted to perform a given task. Now they say: "I went through high school" or "I went through college." That doesn't mean anything. But if they said they are a machinist, a chemist or a cabinetmaker, that does mean something.[16]

February 24, 1930, *Time*

[Schools] do not teach enough things and not enough about each thing. They should teach more about more things. They're particularly bad on history.[17]

July 30, 1930, *New York Times*

A man who cannot think is not an educated man, no matter how many college degrees he has.[18]

October 30, 1930, *Harper's Magazine*

Let the public schools teach children to read and write. Then industry should take them up.[19]

March 17, 1931, *New York Times*

Education can not make a child appreciate life, so much as life can make him appreciate education.[20]

October 1934, *Good Housekeeping*

A car must run well over all sorts of roads and in all kinds of weathers; the educated person must be able to adjust himself to whatever conditions he finds around him.[21]

October 1934, *Good Housekeeping*

One of the reasons there are so many theories is that the value of any method cannot be measured until the generation under which it was educated has grown up. Then it's too late to make changes.[22]

January 12, 1936, *New York Times*

As a matter of fact, it isn't really necessary to *teach* children. All you need to do is let them learn.[23]

September 1938, *Reader's Digest*

On Books, Reading, Literature, and Poetry

If you read, read what is good and get all the good there is in it. Read to get your own conception of the author's meaning, and do some thinking on your own account.[24]

January 25, 1919, *New York Times*

I myself rarely read anything else except the headlines of any article.[25]

July 19, 1919, *New York Tribune*

I am not a very fast reader, and I have the hay fever, and I would make a botch of it. . . . I can read.[26]

July 23, 1919, *New York Times*, response to a question about his ability to read

I'd rather have [a first-edition McGuffey Reader] than a railroad.[27]

October 23, 1921, *New York Times*

Emerson is a pup. . . . Well, I just get comfortably settled down to reading of him when he uses a word I do not understand, and that makes me get up and look for a dictionary.[28]

Circa 1923

I don't like to read books. They muss up my mind.[29]

Circa 1923

The best thing a book can do for a man is to teach him how to think. It isn't what you get out of the book, but what a book pulls out of you that makes it useful.[30]

Circa 1928

I read poetry and I enjoy it if it says anything but so often it doesn't say anything.[31]

July 30, 1930, *New York Times*

Our reading is too casual. We read to escape thinking. Reading can become a dope habit. . . . Booksickness is a modern ailment.[32]

October 1930, *Harper's Magazine*

But as between the steam engine and the book, it was the engine that changed the entire economic system.[33]

June 1936, *Rotarian*

Literature is all right but it doesn't mean much.[34]

April 21, 1947, *Time*

On Writing

I do it in my head.[35]

Date unknown

On Art

Art is something I know nothing about.[36]

Date unknown

But, gentlemen, what would I want with the original pictures when the ones right here in these books are so beautiful?[37]

Circa 1920, comment to a dejected art dealer who had provided Ford with a portfolio of works for sale

You say Rembrandt died of starvation because nobody would buy his pictures? Well, I wouldn't have bought them. I believe things should be artistic, but to be artistic they must be useful as well as beautiful.[38]

May 11, 1926, *Boston Daily Globe*

[E]very inch of his work is technically correct. That's what is so amazing![39]

Circa 1933, regarding the work of the painter Diego Rivera

On Music

I do not care for jazz, but I love the old tunes and dances, and it is a delight to see how the children and the old people alike take to them.[40]

October 1934, *American Magazine*

Start the day with a song.[41]

April 1936, *Etude*

11 ⚙ On History, the Past, and Museums

Henry Ford famously said, "History is bunk." As a pacifist, he deplored history taught as a series of military conquests. As he grew older, the automaker became disillusioned with modern life, despite the fact that his automobile, assembly lines, and factories helped so much to bring it about. Industrialization resulted in the relocation of people to cities and suburbs and away from family farms. Automobiles brought speed, highways, and suburbanization. In an attempt to put the technological genie back into the bottle, Henry Ford established the Edison Institute, later called Greenfield Village. Ford considered Greenfield Village, a collection of relocated historic buildings and artifacts, to be one of the crowning achievements of his life because it brought American history directly to the people.

History is more or less bunk. It's tradition. We don't want tradition. We want to live in the present and the only history worth a tinker's dam is the history we make today.[1]

May 25, 1916, *Chicago Tribune*

I did not say it was bunk. It was bunk to me.[2]

Circa 1916

Henry Ford and Francis Jehl watch Thomas Edison as he re-creates experiments in his Menlo Park Laboratory at the Lights Golden Jubilee, October 21, 1929. Ford relocated the New Jersey laboratory to Michigan to include it in the Edison Institute, which opened to the public in 1933. Today it is part of the Henry Ford Museum and Greenfield Village. Courtesy of the Thomas Edison National Historic Park, 14.140.15.

No. I don't know anything about history, and I wouldn't give a nickel for all the history of the world.[3]

November 1916, *Current Opinion*

Besides, history is being rewritten every year from a new point of view; so how can anybody claim to know the truth about history?[4]

November 1916, *Current Opinion*

We should be guiding our future by the present, instead of being guided in the present by the past.[5]

Circa 1917

Now, I say history is bunk—bunk—double bunk. Why it isn't even true. They wrote what they wanted us to believe, glorifying some conqueror or leader or something like that.[6]

January 1922, *Hearst's International*

The old world is dead, dead, dead. It is beyond recovery. God himself will not restore it, and Satan cannot. . . . The old era is dead, and is being buried bit by bit. Every day another fragment of it falls to dust.[7]

Circa 1922

Rome is still there. People are still living there, aren't they?[8]

February 12, 1924, *Boston Daily Globe*, response to a question about the fall of the Roman Empire

Some history is bunk.[9]

February 12, 1924, *New York Times*

I understand there was one in 1812.[10]

Circa February 1924, response to a question about the American Revolution

I have forgotten just who he is. He is a writer, I think.[11]

Circa February 1924, response to a question about Benedict Arnold

I like old things.[12]

August 16, 1925, *New York Times*

An antique is not valuable because it cost much money, but because of its meaning.[13]

August 16, 1925, *New York Times*

Besides, the further a boy is able to look back, the further he can look ahead.[14]

Circa 1928

Anything that has passed, is all right, in my opinion. Perhaps it had to come in order to pass. I don't quarrel with the past.[15]

Circa 1928

[T]he old world's gone, and it's not coming back. I suppose we should be glad of that. But, as I get older, I miss some of the old ways.[16]

Circa 1932

This talk about going back is foolish. Back to what? To the old-time wood-burning cook stove? To roads deep in mud? To the oil lamp? To the horse and buggy? Yes, I have heard people talk about going back, but they never say what we are going back to.[17]

July 1933, *Good Housekeeping*

There are only two things I know of that we might go back to. One is the single-room schoolhouse in small communities, and the other is back to the land.[18]

July 1933, *Good Housekeeping*

It's all well enough to dig back into the past. We can learn from its mistakes and its victories, but we can't do anything about it.[19]

October 1934, *Good Housekeeping*

Whatever is produced today has something in it of everything that has gone before.[20]

January 12, 1936, *New York Times*

[W]hen I was a boy many people worked in their own homes. A romantic notion about this has grown up. But, as a matter of hard fact, men, women and children lived in workshops. They had no real homes.[21]

July 25, 1943, *New York Times*

I've got a lot of money, and I'd give every penny of it right now just to be here with Mrs. Ford the same as I was in the old days.[22]

Circa 1943–47, in reference to his old farmhouse

History as sometimes written is mostly bunk. But history that you can see is of great value.[23]

April 8, 1947, *Toledo (Ohio) Blade*

On the Henry Ford Museum, Greenfield Village, and Museums

When we are through we shall have reproduced American life as lived in the past, and that, I think, is the best way of preserving a part of our history and tradition.[24]

Circa 1920–29

I don't like "dead" museums.[25]

Circa 1928

When we are through we shall have reproduced American life as lived; and that, I think, is the best way of preserving at least a part of our history and tradition. For by looking at things that people used and that show the way they lived, a better and truer impression can be gained than could be had in a month of reading—even if there were books whose authors had the facilities to discover the minute details of the older life.[26]

April 5, 1931, *New York Times*

We're going to build a museum that's going to show industrial history, and it won't be bunk.[27]

Circa 1931–39

A piece of machinery or anything that is made is like a book, if you can read it. It is part of the record of man's spirit.[28]

January 12, 1936, *New York Times*, on the educational value of the artifacts in his museum

Pack it up and ship it to Dearborn.[29]

Circa 1936–39. Ford purchased antiques en masse, sometimes the inventory of an entire store.

This museum and all connected with it, is for the inspiration of youth.[30]

Circa 1940–47

12 ⚙ On the Press

Henry Ford appreciated the press when it promoted his home-spun image and his business interests. He criticized the media when it depicted him negatively. Surprisingly, he sometimes gave reporters carte blanche access and told them to print whatever they liked. Whether positive or negative, the attention of the press severely limited his privacy and sometimes made him feel as if he was under siege.

In 1919, Ford purchased the existing *Dearborn Independent* as a conduit for his personal views. Very soon the paper's anti-Semitic articles became controversial. The *Dearborn Independent* was closed in December 1927 as part of the Sapiro defamation settlement.[1]

Newspapers have power to end war, for it is through publicity that the gospel of peace is spread.[2]
December 30, 1915, *Toledo (Ohio) Blade*

As to that, fix it any way you like. You will anyway.[3]
January 4, 1916, *New York Times*, comment to a reporter

I would suppress about half of [newspapers] tomorrow. I would have the Government hire a page in every newspaper in the United States and make the newspaper print the record of Congress every day so that the people could find out what's going on down there.[4]
May 24, 1916, *Boston Daily Globe*

I'll give you an interview if you can spell Muscle Shoals for me.[5]

> Circa 1923, reaction to reporters who had not done their homework on his proposed hydroelectric project

Now you go and write anything you please and sign my name to it. I will not repudiate it, whatever you write. I will certify that you saw me.[6]

> Circa 1923. Despite his complaints about the press, Ford's largess was sometimes extreme.

You fellows are a darned nuisance.[7]

> December 4, 1925, *New York Times*, response to reporters asking him to pose for photographs

I don't want to talk with you any more until you've learned something.[8]

> January 7, 1928, *Literary Digest*, response to a reporter who suggested his assembly-line employees worked like robots

With his back against the wall, Henry Ford is interviewed by the press, December 2, 1915. Courtesy of the Library of Congress, B2-3689-1.

I'll listen to you, but there's no use of talking when we can't understand each other.[9]

January 7, 1928, *Literary Digest*

I have nothing to say. I have been misquoted all over Europe and intend to say nothing for publication until I reach Dearborn, where I can protect myself.[10]

October 23, 1930, *New York Times*

The damned rotten newspapers are making me look that way.[11]

Circa 1930–31, response to Thomas Edison's criticism of his anti-Semitic statements

[T]hey're all a bunch of skunks, and you know what happens to people who play with skunks.[12]

Circa 1930–39, on reporters

On the *Dearborn Independent*

I have definite ideas and ideals that I believe are practical for the good of all. I intend giving them to the public without having them garbled, distorted and misrepresented.[13]

November 23, 1918, *New York Times*

The *Dearborn Independent*, an organ of unbiased opinion.[14]

Circa 1920–27, Ford's slogan for the *Independent*

The thought came to me like a flash. Surely some place in the United States there should be a publisher strong and courageous enough to tell people the truth about war. If no one else will I'll turn publisher myself. And I did.[15]

December 5, 1921, *New York Times*

Shut the thing down completely and throw out the machinery.[16]

July 18, 1927, *Time*, on the demise of the *Dearborn Independent*

13 ⚙ On Humanity

Ford was generally optimistic about his fellow human beings, genially reporting, "People are all right." He felt that old men contributed a great deal to society and that young people were the hope of humanity. Many of Ford's pronouncements about men reflect his opinions on humanity in general.

The automaker respected women and felt they did not receive enough credit for their work in the home. Though he believed women's work should be limited to the domestic sphere, Ford employed female workers at his Phoenix Village Industry Plant and in lesser numbers at other plants. Those factories generally employed only single women or married women with disabled husbands.

People never disappoint you if you trust them.[1]

Circa 1917

A man can't afford to look out for himself at the expense of any one else, because anything that hurts the other man is bound to hurt you in the end, in some way.[2]

Circa 1917

Any man who considers everything from the standpoint of the most good to the most people will never want for anything.[3]

Circa 1917

This whole world is like a machine—every part is as important as every other part. We should all work together, not against each other. Anything that is good for all the parts of the machine is good for each one of them.[4]

Circa 1917

I tell you, loyalty, and friendliness, and helping the other man along are the only really valuable things in this world, and they bring all "practical" advantages along with them every time. If every one of us had the courage to believe that, and act on it, war and waste and misery of all kinds would be wiped out over night.[5]

Circa 1917

Henry Ford, Thomas Edison, and botanist Luther Burbank surrounded by a crowd in Santa Rosa, California, 1915. Courtesy of the Thomas Edison National Historic Park, 14.130.100.

Human nature is essentially selfish.[6]

September 1918, *World's Work*

When a man's hands are callused and women's hands are worn, you may be sure honesty is there. That's more than you can say about many soft white hands.[7]

Circa May 24, 1919

Everybody wants to be someplace he ain't. As soon as he gets there he wants to go right back.[8]

Circa 1920–29

[W]e accept the majority of people because we do not know them; the majority of those we avoid are the ones whom we know.[9]

Circa 1922

There are always two kinds of people in the world—those who pioneer and those who plod. The plodders always attack the pioneers. They say that the pioneers have gobbled up all the opportunity, when, as a plain matter of fact, the plodders would have nowhere to plod had not the pioneers first cleared the way.[10]

Circa 1926

A man is like a well. There is a vast amount of him, if he can only get it out.[11]

Circa 1928

When people become too contented, there's usually trouble ahead.[12]

May 29, 1930, *New York Times*

It is only man that progresses.[13]

September 13, 1931, *New York Times*

The pessimist says our experience is not going to teach us anything. He says the human race never learns anything; it just stumbles from one panic to another. I am an optimist on that point—I think we have all learned a lot.[14]

November 8, 1931, *New York Times*

On Men

The sign of a little man is so various that it is next to impossible for an ordinarily observant person to mistake him. He never forgets himself. He is afraid to surround himself with bigger men than himself, with men who know more, or can give him help. Thus the little man is a fool.[15]

Circa 1922

Men are not divided by the kind of work they do, but by the kind of men they are.[16]

Circa 1922

Perhaps it is true that the majority of men need the restraint of public opinion.[17]

Circa 1923

I have never met a man who was thoroughly bad. There is always some good in him—if he gets a chance.[18]

Circa 1923

More men are beaten than fail.[19]

Circa 1923

The whole world's run by mediocre men, you know. The bright men can't run the world alone. You've got to have the dumbells [*sic*] with 'em.[20]

May 11, 1926, *Boston Daily Globe*

Man can do whatever he can imagine.[21]

Circa 1940–45

Men are not so predictable as principles, there is always doubt.[22]

August 1942, *Rotarian*

On Women

To say it plainly, the great majority of women who work do so in order to buy fancy clothes.[23]

Circa 1922

Every great man has had a great wife behind him.[24]

September 1923, *Ladies' Home Journal*

Nagging is as effective in making a man get the best out of himself as loving consideration. Sometimes more so. We have punished women for nagging; we have criticized them severely for it; but it is about time to do justice to the instinct of which this is the outward sign.[25]

September 1923, *Ladies' Home Journal*

The woman who is constantly advising her family and shielding them from hurt only weakens them in the end.[26]

September 1923, *Ladies' Home Journal*

I have given women every chance to develop in our organization. I don't know why it is, but they don't get very far.[27]

September 1923, *Ladies' Home Journal*

I consider women only a temporary factor in industry. Their real job in life is to get married, have a home and raise a family. I pay our women well so they can dress attractively and get married.[28]

September 1923, *Ladies' Home Journal*

[W]e do not employ married women whose husbands have jobs.[29]

Circa 1923

The women today are calmer than the men. They have more faith, more patience. They know the men will work out these troubles. They expect us to; and since civilization began, men have done what women expected of them.[30]

July 1933, *Good Housekeeping*

I'll bet a woman got you into it.[31]

Circa 1940–47, standard comment when he talked with ex-convicts about their crimes

Don't ever discredit the power of a woman.[32]

Circa 1941, comment regarding his wife's effective threat to divorce him if he did not negotiate with the union

It lifts the standards of the [factory] shop to have women in it. It always does. I am glad they are here. They make better men out of our workers. Whenever there are women in industry, they lift the standard of the workers.[33]

September 1944, *Rotarian*. During World War II, with men off to war, Ford factories hired more women.

The women in the home do not get half the credit that is due them. The man stands out in front. His success is talked about. He gets the fame, but the woman who stood by him in difficult times deserves a lot of credit for his success.[34]

January 1947, *Rotarian*

On Marriage

A wife helps a man more than any one else. She criticizes him more.[35]

Circa 1917

If a man leaves the house in the morning after an angry word with his wife he has practically ruined his day and hers too. He ought to go back and fix up the strained relations.[36]

Circa 1922

Love of the pretty sort may be absent from that partnership; but if there is friendship, if there are faith and courage and a devotion to something higher than material things, that marriage has been worth while.[37]

September 1923, *Ladies' Home Journal*

No man can expect to be anything or get anywhere unless he has a good wife. One of the first aims of a young man out of school should be to get married.[38]

February 24, 1930, *Time*

On Parenting

All that the child requires from the parent is to be brought to the age of usefulness and to be given an opportunity to work out his own destiny.[39]

December 4, 1921, *Boston Daily Globe*

Don't try to do too much for your child. Your job is to help him help himself, not to help him shun social responsibility.[40]

Circa 1930–39

On Age and Aging

Why, I never think of diminishing days. I'm living in today, not tomorrow or yesterday. Yesterday has been taken care of and tomorrow will take care of itself.[41]

July 30, 1925, *Boston Daily Globe*

They talk about young men nowadays, but old men are the best. They can't skip around so fast, but they have experience behind them.[42]

May 11, 1926, *Boston Daily Globe*

Take all the experience and judgment of men over 50 out of the world, and there would not be enough left to run it. Youngsters have their place and are necessary but the experience and judgment of men over 50 are what gives purpose and meaning to younger men's efforts.[43]

July 31, 1928, *New York Times*

Up to the age of forty, a man is in training—every man is.[44]

July 1928, *American Magazine*

Age has nothing to do with years, but with the vigor of mind and body.[45]

Circa 1928

I don't believe in age limits.[46]

Circa 1928

Fifty used to be old age. Now it is just maturity.[47]

Circa 1928

Anyone who stops learning is old—whether this happens at twenty or at eighty. Anyone who keeps learning stays young. The greatest thing in life is to keep your mind young.[48]

July 1929, *Ladies' Home Journal*

By ox strength and stupidity youth sometimes elbows experience out of the way, but experience wins finally. It is the only practical guide we can rely upon.[49]

July 1933, *Good Housekeeping*

Until a man is forty he is learning how to learn. After forty he learns and begins to apply his knowledge. Experience. That's his finest asset.[50]

July 1933, *Good Housekeeping*

The secret of growing old without knowing it is to keep on working.[51]

July 30, 1936, *New York Times*

On Youth and Advice to Youth

Children are the last production of Heaven and the best; they get better the more they turn out![52]

Circa 1923

The average boy is honest, but also if he is normal he is mischievous.[53]

December 1926, *World's Work*

They are no crazier to-day than they ever were—it may be that they have more sense than they used to. Certainly the girls have more sense, for they have more freedom and thus greater opportunity to gain sense. Some people seem to think that they dress queerly and act queerly.[54]

December 1926, *World's Work*

Our hope is the new generation. They accept new things more readily, because they have no false education, no preconceived ideas to reverse.[55]

Circa 1928

[T]oday's youngsters are a fine lot and they decidedly are not headed for perdition.[56]

May 30, 1930, *New York Times*

Youth and age need each other.[57]

May 30, 1930, *New York Times*

Youth has no preconceived notions.[58]

August 9, 1931, *New York Times*

If our young men are to do our fighting, why can't they run the country? . . . [F]or the old heads have made a botch of things in many quarters.[59]

March 12, 1941, *New York Times*

If you want to keep up with the times, learn from the children and from youth. They are the last production of destiny—and the best.[60]

January 1947, *Rotarian*

I'd rather take the advice of a child than that of nine-tenths of the grownups in this world.[61]

January 1947, *Rotarian*

A young man ought to . . . look for the single spark of individuality that makes him different from other folks, and develop that for all he's worth.[62]

Date unknown

14 ⚙ On Religion, Reincarnation, and Charity

Ford was raised Episcopalian. Though he did not often attend services, he felt his employees should. He believed that the Bible should be taught in schools, but he also expressed the view that only two of its books were "worth a damn."[1]

Ford's ambivalence was not uncommon. Like many in his generation, he was caught between a loyalty to traditional Christian beliefs and disillusionment resulting from war and scientific theories, like evolution, which seemed to contradict religion. Before the turn of the century, for reasons that are unclear, Ford began to believe in reincarnation and spoke publicly on the topic. Perhaps he felt the philosophy offered validation for his many accomplishments. As he grew older, Ford thought his own success was a result of destiny.

As for charity, the automaker thought it was a waste, an insult to the recipient, and a way for the givers to entertain a false sense of their own benevolence. Ironically, today the Ford Foundation, an independent philanthropic organization established by Edsel Ford in 1936, donates millions to charity.

Henry Ford, circa 1919. Courtesy of the Library of Congress, LC-USZ62-111278.

I want you, Mark, to put Jesus Christ in my factory![2]

Circa 1915, request that Rev. Samuel Simpson Marquis work in the Sociological Division of the Ford Motor Company

Miracles are only the aspirations of the many carried out by the few.[3]

December 11, 1915, *Literary Digest*

I see no use in spending a great deal of time learning about heaven and hell. In my opinion, a man makes his own heaven and hell and carries it around with him. Both are states of mind.[4]

Circa 1917

Oh, no, I am not orthodox in my religion. Doing for your fellow-men is religion enough for me.[5]

October 29, 1922, *New York Times*

The only thing that I can see that is wrong with the Bible is that it isn't read enough any more, especially in the schools.[6]

April 1924, *Good Housekeeping*

The trouble with you preachers is that you keep insisting upon calling the Bible the "sacred book" all the time. If you stopped using that phrase, more people would read the Bible. You drive them away from it by calling it sacred, by setting it up on a pedestal away from the common people. You make them afraid of it.[7]

April 1924, *Good Housekeeping*

But would Isaiah be writing more Bible today? . . . He would probably be down in the shops among the workmen; working over a set of blueprints; remaking the world rather than writing about it. There is no reason why a prophet should not be an engineer instead of a preacher.[8]

April 1924, *Good Housekeeping*

Church should be made attractive. Perhaps I am over enthusiastic about square dances, old-fashioned dances; but it seems to me that therein the church can find much to attract youth. A good dancing master, a good fiddler and a good floor will do very much more to attract a young congregation than all the lectures in the world.[9]

August 16, 1925, *New York Times*

People who fight against religion haven't much religion to fight about.[10]

October 31, 1925, *New York Times*

I think the real power of human lives is hidden away in the soul, and farther than that. There are actual entities all around us, entities of force, intelligence—call them electrons, if you like. When man is doing good, they swarm to help him.[11]

Circa 1926. Ford's belief in "entities" was influenced by Thomas Edison.

If one meditates too much there is not likely to be much work done![12]

Circa 1926

Somewhere there is a Master Mind which sends brain waves or messages to us—the Brain of Mankind, the Brain of the Earth. There is a Great Spirit. Call it Creative Evolution or World Mind. Call it Collective Intelligence or call it God. It is this Spirit which determines our actions and our thoughts. . . . I adopted the theory of reincarnation when I was twenty-six. I got the idea from a book by Orlando Smith.[13] Until I discovered this theory, I was unsettled and dissatisfied—without a compass, so to speak.

If you preserve a record of this conversation, write it so that it puts men's minds at ease. I would like to communicate to others the calmness that the long view of life gives to us.[14]

September 3, 1928, *Time*

I look upon the Bible as a record of experience. No matter what knocks we receive in life, we find, reading the Bible, that others have received similar knocks. It is a true book of experience.[15]

September 3, 1928, *Time*

Every man works out his own religion, if he gives it any attention at all.[16]

Circa 1928

Personally, I don't see how any one can escape getting good from going to church. But I do not go often myself.[17]

Circa 1928

What we call "belief" now, was once knowledge.[18]

Circa 1928

Another of my beliefs is that we are in contact with all about us, that we ourselves are a universe in miniature, with the self as the center and numberless millions of entities making up the thing we call "I"; that we function not only on the planes we see, but on others that we do not see; that we are ourselves little universes coming to consciousness, trying to recall powers and knowledge we once had.[19]

Circa 1928

To my mind, natural law and spiritual law are one and the same—no difference.[20]

Circa 1928

Religion is like electricity. I do not understand electricity, but I am deeply interested in it. I want to know all I can about it. I know that it warms our hearts and that it makes the world better. I know that it lights the dark places of the earth. I see and admit its effectiveness even though I do not profess to understand it at all.[21]

July 25, 1929, *New York Times*

There are only two things in the Book worth a damn.[22]

Circa 1930–39, Ford's opinion of the Bible. His exceptions were Paul's declaration of faith to the Romans and Hebrews chapter 11.

Well, now you've got the best religion in the world.[23]

Circa 1930–39, comment made to clergymen of all denominations who visited Ford

I'm guided, Harry, I'm guided.[24]

Circa 1940–47, expressing his belief that his decisions were inspired by God

All men in their hearts are spiritual. Some, however, try to buck it.[25]

July 25, 1943, *New York Times*

If you truely [*sic*] ask to be Guided you will be led in every move you make.[26]

Date unknown, from one of Ford's personal notebooks

On Reincarnation

Oh, you mean reincarnation. You believe that? I do, too.[27]

Date unknown

Everything is indestructible, nothing is ever lost. Souls come and go, and they come again, prepared by past experience for greater achievement.[28]

Circa 1926

I adopted the theory of Reincarnation when I was twenty-six. Religion offered nothing to the point. Even work could not give me complete satisfaction. Work is futile if we cannot utilize the experience we collect in one life in the next. When I discovered Reincarnation it was as if I had found a universal plan. I realized that there was a chance to work out my ideas. Time was no longer limited. I was no longer a slave to the clock. Genius is experience. Some seem to think that it is a gift of talent, but it is the fruit of long experience in many lives. Some are older souls than others, and so they know more. The discovery of Reincarnation put my mind at ease.[29]

August 26, 1928, *San Francisco Examiner*

As I have said, my belief is that Jesus was an old person, old in experience; and it was this that gave him his superior knowledge of life.[30]

Circa 1928

When I discovered reincarnation it was as if I found a universal plan. I realized that there was a chance to work out any ideas. Time was no longer a limit.[31]

Circa 1930–39

We are here to work out something, and we go on from where we leave off. That's my religion, though I was brought up an Episcopalian. For myself, I'm certain that I have lived before, that I stored up considerable experience before the present stage, and that I will proceed to the next stage when this is finished. It's all trial-and-error, but based, I guess, on certain fundamentals.[32]

May 29, 1932, *New York Times*

When the automobile was new and one of them came down the road, a chicken would run straight for home—and usually get killed. But today when a car comes along, a chicken will run for the nearest side of the road. That chicken has been hit in the ass in a previous life.[33]

Circa 1940–47, proof of reincarnation

You know, when a person dies I think their spirit goes into a new-born baby. I think that's why some people are so much further advanced in knowledge than others and are gifted. A man when he dies, if he is a genius, his spirit will go into a newborn baby and that person will be an expert like Einstein or Edison.[34]

Circa 1940–47

I never did anything by my own volition. . . . I was pushed by invisible forces within and without me. We inherit a native knowledge from a previous experience.[35]

Circa 1940–47

[Y]ou know my belief—Edsel isn't dead.[36]

Circa 1943–44, statement following the death of his son

On Superstition

If a black cat crosses the road and you're superstitious, then you drive more carefully, and that's a good thing. Anyone who will walk under a ladder deserves to get a paint pot on his head.[37]

Date unknown

On Charity, Philanthropy, and Welfare

I have been accused of being a philanthropist. I am not. I am an ardent believer in the gospel of good will.[38]

Circa 1914

A man with a program is like a dead fish floating down a stream.[39]

Circa 1917

Everybody helps me. If I'm going to do my part I must help everybody![40]

Circa 1917

I'm off charity for life.[41]

November 19, 1918, *Boston Daily Globe*

Americans do not want charity, anyhow. All they want is a chance to work for their living, and I will give more of them than ever a chance to do so.[42]

November 19, 1918, *Boston Daily Globe*

Society does not owe any man a living, but society does owe him a chance to work.[43]

Circa 1920–29

I don't believe in philanthropy. And as for charity, there is no such thing. You're self-supporting, I'm self-supporting, and there is no reason why everybody shouldn't be self-supporting. If you give charity you lessen the chances of doing away with poverty.[44]

July 29, 1921, *New York Times*

Charity lowers the self-respect of the person who receives it and it deadens the conscience of the person who gives it.[45]

Circa 1921

For that is really what we do in most of our makeshift charity—we simply ease our own pain at the sight of suffering.[46]

Circa 1921

The best charity we know anything about is to help a man to the place where he will never need it.[47]

Circa 1921

Whole sections of our population were coddled into the habit of expecting something, as children do.[48]

Circa 1922

Whoever offers charity, offers insult.[49]

November 14, 1923, *New Republic*

It is easy to give; it is harder to make giving unnecessary.[50]
Circa 1923

No man ever helped another by giving money.[51]
Circa 1923

If you want to make any one your enemy, hand him something for nothing.[52]
Circa 1923

Philanthropy? Philanthropy? No. No.[53]
March 5, 1927, *Literary Digest*, on what he would do with his fortune

Endowment is an opiate to imagination, a drug to initiative. Inertia and smug satisfaction invariably follow. One of the great curses of the country today is the practice of endowing this and endowing that.[54]
April 8, 1947, *Toledo (Ohio) Blade*

Never give anything without strings attached to it.[55]
Date unknown

Aid the man who sweats.[56]
Date unknown

On Poverty and the Poor

You have seen two fellows on a street corner. Both of them are down and out; but one has ten cents. With that he can buy a bun and a bed for himself. Or he can buy a bun for himself and a bun for his chum, and take chances on getting a bed. If he does that he is my kind of folks.[57]
May 29, 1915, *Harper's Weekly*

I want to abolish poverty in America. I want to make a good home possible for every child. Low wages are silly. You can't get rich by making people poor. They can't buy your goods and there you are.[58]

Circa 1923

Why, it wouldn't discourage me a bit to go broke. In some ways it would be fun to go out in the world again and struggle as I once did. I wouldn't mind a bit; I wouldn't mind it a bit.[59]

Circa 1923

On Reform and Reformers

The man who calls himself a reformer wants to smash things. He is the sort of man who could tear up a whole shirt because the collar button did not fit the button hole. It would never occur to him to enlarge the hole. This sort of reformer never under any circumstances knows what he is doing. Experience and reform do not go together. A reformer cannot keep his zeal at white heat in the presence of fact. He must discard all facts.[60]

Circa 1923

15 ⚙ On Nations, Nationalities, Ethnic and Religious Groups, and the United States

Henry Ford's opinions of nations and ethnic and religious groups were influenced by his own prejudices. Though he advocated tolerance, Ford was distrustful of ethnic minorities, especially Jews and non-English speakers. English schools in his plants promoted complete assimilation. At graduation, employees dressed in the clothing of their native lands entered an enormous "melting pot," only to emerge transformed, in American-style clothing.

As discussed in the preface, the section "On Jews" is not a list of quotes, but rather a chronicle of Ford's opinions and actions regarding Jews.

Ford considered the United States the best nation in the world, and as such, her people were the world's most fortunate. He found much serenity in his beloved Michigan but also owned vacation homes in Fort Myers, Florida, and Richmond Hill, Georgia.

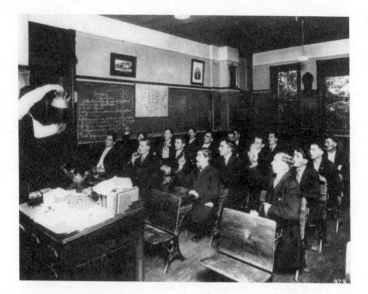

Ford's English School at the Highland Park Plant, circa 1914–15. At the Ford English School, employees learned English and American customs, as well as the virtues of thrift, industriousness, and cleanliness. From the Collections of the Henry Ford, THF23827.

On Race

Race differences? They do not exist in sufficient degree to make men fight, and they are disappearing every day. See how the races mix in America! I have fifty-three nationalities, speaking more than one hundred different languages and dialects, in my shops, and they never have any trouble.[1]

Circa 1917

On Tolerance

I don't care what they are: Hungarians, Austrians, Germans. As long as they work for me and do a good job, they're all right with me.[2]

Circa 1917

Tolerance is possible only to the superior; the lower elements are always intolerant.[3]

Circa 1922

The Lord has tolerated these creeds. Why cannot the people?[4]

June 23, 1923, *New York Times*, response to a question about Mexican Catholics

We are beginning to see that you can't build anything permanent on hate. The world is learning tolerance as never before.[5]

January 1947, *Rotarian*

On Immigrants and Americanization

These men of many nations must be taught American ways, the English language, the right way to live.[6]

April 19, 1914, *New York Times*

What of the Melting Pot? . . . The problem is not . . . with the pot so much as with the base metal. Some metals cannot be assimilated, refuse to mix with the molten mass of the citizenship, but remain ugly, undissoluble [*sic*] lumps.[7]

February 22, 1919, *Dearborn Independent*

On African Americans

No friend of mine goes in the back door.[8]

Circa 1942, said to the black scientist George Washington Carver

On Catholics

Oh, he isn't a *good* Catholic.[9]
Circa 1930–39, response when asked if he liked someone who was Catholic

[Catholics are] tools of the Jews.[10]
Circa 1930–39

On China

China will also readjust herself when the people learn to want more things, the necessities of life and even some luxuries, and when they know that there is no other way of getting these things than by hard work.[11]
November 21, 1927, *New York Times*

On England and the English

I never heard a cross word, the English being the kindest and quietest people I have ever met.[12]
December 1, 1915, *New York Times*

On Europe

One of the greatest troubles with Europe is that the people exist for the Government.[13]
February 25, 1924, *New York Times*

You know, the brains left those old countries and much of the brains came here when this country was settled.[14]
May 11, 1926, *Boston Daily Globe*

On France

In France everybody is working, but it does not take much to keep them busy.[15]

October 17, 1930, *New York Times*

On Germans

The Germans would have been better off if they had had eyes like the woodcock. The woodcock has eyes so near the back of his head that he can see behind.[16]

November 14, 1923, *New Republic*

On Ireland and the Irish

There is no Irish question today and we would hear little trouble there if the newspapers didn't magnify every little thing that happens there.[17]

August 20, 1924, *Boston Daily Globe*

On Jews

Henry Ford spent most of his adult life waging a war of words against Jews. Historians have struggled to discover the cause of his fixation. In interviews and in books published in his name, he referred to Jews as "kikes"[18] and "money maniacs."[19] He collectively blamed Jews for World Wars I and II, the Depression, alcoholism, organized crime, jazz, and general societal degeneracy. Further, Ford claimed Jews controlled the banks, theater, press, the presidency, and indeed, planned to dominate the world.

He made anti-Semitic comments to family, friends, neighbors, business associates, and the press throughout his adult life. Most were along the lines of a remark he made in a *New Republic* interview: "Wherever there's anything wrong with a country, you'll find the Jews on the job there."[20]

In 1919, he began publication of his own newspaper, the *Dearborn Independent*. The paper's first editor quit over the anti-Semitic articles and warned, "[I]f Ford ever gets into power, look out!"[21] Under its new editor, William Cameron, the *Independent* printed the series "The International Jew: The World's Problem." Articles such as "Jewish Jazz—Moron Music—Becomes Our National Music" blamed Jews for corrupting American society.

Issues of the newspaper from the early 1920s were compiled into four pamphlets entitled *The International Jew: The World's Foremost Problem,* with Henry Ford listed as author. Chapters like "Jewish Degradation of American Baseball" and "Jewish Hot-Beds of Bolshevism in the U.S." accused Jews of debasing American culture. More than a half million copies of *The International Jew* were distributed through Ford dealerships.[22] The pamphlets were also circulated worldwide with translated editions in German, Russian, and other languages.

Between 1920 and 1922, the *Dearborn Independent* published the so-called "Protocols of the Elders of Zion." The document, which purported to disclose plans for Jewish world domination, was a well-established forgery.[23] Nevertheless, by publishing and distributing it, Henry Ford gave credence to anti-Jewish paranoia.

Ford's opinions and publications offended many. Presidents Wilson and Taft and President-elect Harding joined other prominent Americans in publicly condemning him.[24] Ford's own wife and son withdrew their names and support from the *Dearborn Independent* in 1923.[25]

Others, unfortunately, were impressed. The German translation of *The International Jew* was popular with Nazis. In 1931, Adolph Hitler told a Detroit reporter, "I regard Henry Ford as my inspiration."[26] Indeed, Ford's picture hung on the wall of Hitler's Munich office, and the dictator awarded Ford the Grand Cross of the German Eagle in 1938.

Despite his rants, Ford personally admired a number of Jewish individuals, including his Detroit neighbor Rabbi Leo Franklin, and the architect of his Highland Park plant, Albert Kahn. Jewish songwriter and former Ford employee Irving Caesar counted himself as a friend. Caesar confronted Ford about violence against Jews perpetrated in his name; he asserted that Ford never "really realized the enormity of his error."[27]

Less forgiving was Aaron Sapiro, the leader of a California fruit-growers cooperative. After being attacked in Ford's book *The International Jew*, Sapiro sued for libel. When it became clear that Sapiro would win, Ford agreed to write a formal apology and the lawsuit was dropped.[28] Though Ford continued to disparage Jews privately, he never again did it publicly.

On Mexico and Mexicans

The root difficulty is that he has been taught to hate work, the one thing that every one of us should love; by the fact that he never has had a chance to work right, with the right chance for his family and himself; with any hope that he would receive a fair share of the proceeds from his toil. There is the Mexican situation in a nutshell.[29]

April 11, 1915, *New York Times*

Let me invade Mexico with factories and give the people something to do. Then there will be no more war there.[30]

July 26, 1922, *New York Times*

On Russia and Russians

The fact is that poor Russia is at work, but her work counts for nothing. It is not free work.[31]

Circa 1923

When the Russian masses will learn to want more than they have, when they will want white collars, soap, better clothes, better shoes, better living conditions, then they will work harder to get these things, and that will lead to improvements in the life of the workers and the farmers.[32]

November 21, 1927, *New York Times*

On the United States and Americans

America is the greatest land and has the greatest people in the world. We are the pioneer stock of the world, those who dared.[33]

October 29, 1921, *New York Times*

We believe in democracy because we believe that the collective mind is better than any single mind.[34]

Circa 1922

That is the way I feel about America at this time. We have money. We have the richest country on earth. We have raw products. We have room. We have men. We have ideas. We have people. Let us expand. Distrust of our destiny, fear of the future, should have no place in our minds.[35]

Circa 1923

But my observation is that, on the whole, America is a pretty clean and pretty wholesome place to live.[36]

Circa 1928

Under the American system, we believe in the circulation of prosperity.[37]

September 8, 1928, *New York Times*

The prosperity of this country was gained by the hard work and plain living of its people. The principle that every man should take care of himself and be responsible to himself is the foundation of American life.[38]

May 24, 1931, *New York Times*

American people are conservative. They do not run after any new-fangled remedy, and when they do attempt to do anything radical, they want to see it controlled by experience and common sense.[39]

October 20, 1932, *New York Times*

It is rather a startling thought, that except in three or four favored parts of the earth, there is less human liberty today than there was one hundred years ago. Through war and dictatorship whole nations have ceased to be free. That will not occur here, because the American people will not permit it.[40]

February 1, 1936, *Saturday Evening Post*

Our people are made of different stuff.[41]

February 1, 1936, *Saturday Evening Post*

Certainly our people have more than the people of any other country, but they haven't enough for Americans![42]

October 31, 1936, *Saturday Evening Post*

Except for idealists there would be no United States.[43]

Circa 1938–39

On Boston, Massachusetts

It is the finest city in the country.[44]

August 11, 1924, *Boston Daily Globe*

On Detroit

A lot of people are staying in Detroit for the same reason that some people like to stay at home—that is where they eat.[45]

December 2, 1932, *New York Times*

They were raising a million dollars to advertise Detroit and bring more people here. I told them the money would be better spent to educate people how to get away from the city.[46]

Circa 1920–29

On Fairlane, Ford's Home in Dearborn, Michigan

Here in the midst of scenes where we were boy and girl and lovers together; here in sight of the cottage which was the first modest home where dreams of the future were dreamed, and air castles that have since come down to earth were built; here among old friends we have known all our lives will the new home be erected.[47]

Circa 1910–19

I like privacy in my home. The people would make it a public park. It is to obtain privacy that any man is entitled to in his own home, that I keep a guard at the gate. . . . Unless I did . . . my place would be overrun by strangers.[48]

Circa 1916

On Fort Myers, Florida

A regional paradise.[49]

May 5, 1914, *Fort Myers (Fla.) Press*

On New York

That's the trouble with people from New York. They don't think anybody is sober.[50]

March 24, 1930, *Time*

On Cities

There is something about a city of a million people which is untamed and threatening. Thirty miles away, happy and contented villages read the ravings of the city![51]

Circa 1923

We shall learn some day that much of what we call "social unrest" has its origin in the unnatural conditions under which men and women live in the city.[52]

Circa 1923

The city takes its food from grocery shelves and its opinions from minds too busy to think.[53]

August 10, 1924, *New York Times*

Cities had better stop piling up their skyscrapers anyway. Everyone knows the interior of the earth is plastic. It's possible to get too much weight upon the surface. It's bound to make a dent.[54]

February 24, 1930, *Time*

On Rural Living

If a man owns a home in the country with a little land about it, he can get on for quite a while without much money, but in the city everything is cash—recreation, everything.[55]

July 1933, *Good Housekeeping*

16 ⚙ On Health

Because he was generally healthy, Henry Ford was skeptical about illnesses and infirmities. He thought most physical ailments were caused by excessive eating, improper diet, or addictive substances, such as tobacco and alcohol. Despite his lack of confidence in medicine, he started his own hospital in 1915. The Henry Ford Hospital offered state-of-the art medical care at affordable prices.

The physician John Harvey Kellogg, who operated the Battle Creek Sanitarium, influenced Ford's ideas on nutrition. Like Kellogg, Ford advocated vegetarianism and whole foods and eschewed stimulants like coffee, alcohol, and sugar. Unlike Kellogg, Ford was not a vegetarian and occasionally went on food binges.

On Health and Illness

Once in a while a little group of cells gets together and takes to growing on its own account, not paying any attention to the rest. That is a cancer.[1]

Circa 1917

I'm never sick because I take lots of exercise, eat lightly and get all the fresh air I need.[2]

Circa 1923

In my experience, a cold usually comes from eating.[3]

Circa 1928

Sunshine and plain food are good doctors.[4]

Circa 1928

As long as people know that they can get cured they will have a good time getting sick; they won't abstain, they won't be temperate.[5]

Circa 1928

On Medicine and Medical Care

I have noticed in dealing with doctors . . . that the matter of sticking to their diagnosis seems to be more important than the fate of the patient.[6]

Circa 1923

Henry Ford Hospital. Courtesy Conrad R. Lam Archives, Henry Ford Health System, Detroit, Michigan.

If the doctors would only work to keep people from becoming sick, instead of curing them after they get sick, they would be inundated with money.[7]

May 11, 1926, *Boston Daily Globe*

For forty years, every time I think of it, I rub around my eyes. If you would do that, you would never need glasses.[8]

Circa 1938–45

On Hospitals and the Henry Ford Hospital

I'll give Detroit the best hospital in the world if you'll all get out and let me build it and run it.[9]

September 1918, *World's Work*

It is my shop where I hope people can get well as rapidly as possible and have their injured parts repaired.[10]

Circa 1920–26

But I never believed it right for doctors to regulate the size of their bills by the wealth of their patients. So I decided to build a hospital in which everybody would be charged what the services rendered to him cost and nobody would be charged more.[11]

Circa 1923

The day is coming when a hospital will cease to be thought of as a cure station, and will become a prevention school, a place where people are taught how to live.[12]

Circa 1928

On Food, Eating, and Nutrition

They try to give me fancy food, but I won't stand for it. They can't cook as well as Mrs. Ford either—none of them can.[13]

July 4, 1914, *Collier's*

I am not feeling quite right this morning. I ate some chicken last night for dinner. Chicken is fit only for hawks.[14]

Circa 1923

Meat is not essential. It can be replaced with a scientifically manufactured substitute.[15]

September 14, 1924, *Boston Daily Globe*

We eat no white bread in my house.[16]

August 15, 1924, *New York Times*

I believe that most human ills are directly traceable to food.[17]

February 1925, *Popular Science*

I don't believe in drinking milk for anybody over 8 years old.[18]

May 11, 1926, *New York Times*

I lost nine teeth between the ages of twenty-two and twenty-four from eating too much meat and too much sugar. Since then I have experimented with my diet. I know how much to eat and what to eat. And I've never had a disease.[19]

May 16, 1926, *New York Times*

Most of us eat too much. We eat the wrong kind of food at the wrong time and ultimately suffer for it.[20]

Circa 1928

Five things, I am sure, are injurious. . . . One is sugar. Another is too much starch. Coffee is of no real use, nor tea. Too much wheat is not good for older people. There is no need of meat for food, especially red meat.[21]

Circa 1928

The three errors of diet are eating too little, eating too much, and eating the wrong things. Moderation in food, however, takes the edge off all three errors.[22]

Circa 1928

Well, if I feel a cold coming on, which is rarely, and I want to get over it quickly, I fast for forty-eight hours.[23]

Circa 1928

Yes, salt is one of the best things for teeth. Also for the hair. A couple of teaspoonfuls of salt dissolved in cold water and rubbed into the hair helps keep it vigorous.[24]

Circa 1928

If people would learn to eat the things they should eat, there would be no need for hospitals. Jails and prisons would have less to do.[25]

Circa June 1929

If a good, pure water could be developed to sell at a fair price, there would be a great market for it.[26]

July 31, 1930, *New York Times*

Let's you and I go over to the dining room before the others get there today. I feel like getting drunk—food drunk! Let's go early—now—and eat everything in sight.[27]

Circa 1930–39, on a food binge

You can live as long as you want as long as you only eat cracked wheat.[28]

Circa 1930–39

The time is coming when man will be able to determine the length of his life span by controlling his diet. I think he will find everything he needs in wheat; wheat is the divine food.[29]

Circa June 1944

The fate of the world—the peace of the universe—rests on its breakfast table. . . . Analyze the cause of war and disagreements between individuals. And the answer? You will find it lies in the petty rivalry of dyspeptic statesmen.[30]

Circa 1944–47

On Weight and Obesity

Weight may be desirable in a steam roller, but nowhere else.[31]
Circa 1923

The most beautiful things in the world are those from which all excess weight has been eliminated.[32]
Circa 1923

Cut down on the rations and you won't need doctors. Eat your dessert first and you won't eat so much.[33]
Circa 1923–29

Most men dig their graves with their teeth.[34]
Circa 1923–29

On Alcohol and Prohibition

Well, alcohol is poison. . . . But I don't want people to stop drinking because I tell them to.[35]
November 1916, *Current Opinion*

I think it is one of the causes of the war. . . . Well, alcohol makes people suspicious. I think it made the French and Germans suspicious of each other.[36]
November 1916, *Current Opinion*

I have never tasted liquor in my life. I'd as soon think of taking any other poison.[37]
Circa 1917

Men have sought relief from worry in drink. It's a false refuge.[38]
June 1, 1919, *New York Times*

Booze never did anybody any good in any place at any time.[39]
Circa June 1923

Anyone with a single good eye can see the resulting profit from prohibition without poring over any table or figures.[40]

October 26, 1923, *Boston Daily Globe*

Liquor is as dead as slavery.[41]

Circa 1927

America has improved considerably under prohibition, both industrially and commercially and the rest of the world will follow.[42]

April 11, 1928, *New York Times*

If the prohibition laws were changed we'd have to shut up our plants.[43]

August 18, 1928, *New York Times*

No prosperity is possible unless the country is sober.[44]

November 3, 1928, *New York Times*

But I want to say that if we admit liquor back into the country we are letting in one more ingredient of national poverty.[45]

November 3, 1928, *New York Times*

In common decency the liquor generation should be allowed to die in silence.[46]

Circa 1928

Set a man eating right, and his appetites become normal. He doesn't want liquor.[47]

Circa June 1929

Business and booze are enemies.[48]

Circa July 1929

Gasoline and liquor do not mix. We cannot have liquor and automobiles, too.[49]

Circa July 1929

Prohibition is the greatest experiment yet made to benefit man.[50]

March 6, 1930, *Fort Myers (Fla.) Press*

Do you think I don't know liquor is sold in Dearborn? Of course I know it! It is sold here because the liquor interests are concentrating in this neighborhood because they know I am a dry.[51]

March 24, 1930, *Time*

Brains and booze will not mix.[52]

Circa 1935

On Cigarettes, Smoking, and Tobacco Products

There's a poison in cigarets [*sic*] made by the burning of the paper.[53]

November 1916, *Current Opinion*

If you will study the history of almost any criminal, you will find he is an inveterate cigarette smoker.[54]

Circa 1917

Boys, through cigarettes, train with bad company. They go with other smokers to pool rooms and saloons. The cigarette drags them down.[55]

Circa 1917

17 ⚙ On Nature, Science, Energy, and Fuel

As a young man, Henry Ford detested farmwork and never trusted horses. Part of the rationale behind his automobiles and tractors was to liberate humanity from the burden of fieldwork and animal husbandry. Yet, as the years passed and his automobile began to alter the nation with increased urbanization and suburban sprawl, Ford became nostalgic for family farms. As a result, he established "village industries" to induce factory employees to cultivate the land and, if possible, to live and work in the same small communities.

Henry Ford deplored waste and constantly challenged his employees to find uses for excess materials. He also advocated chemurgy, the process of creating new industrial chemical products from organic raw materials. Ford's best-known chemurgic endeavor was his work with soybeans. Experiments with hundreds of varieties of the Asian plant resulted in high-quality enamel paints for automobiles. He also used soybeans to make gearshift knobs, door handles, and accelerator pedals.[1]

On Animals

The horse will be entirely superseded and, in time, the species will become extinct.[2]

May 3, 1908, *Los Angeles Herald*

So I say in our time we shall look on the horse as a curiosity, an animal only found in zoological gardens and here and there in private herds, like the buffalo herds now owned by a few individuals.[3]

May 3, 1908, *Los Angeles Herald*

I do not believe in caging either animals or birds.[4]

January 12, 1914, *New York Times*

I was never fond of horses in the way that many are. I never really made friends with them.[5]

July 14, 1923, *Literary Digest*

Machine process can manufacture milk more efficiently than the crude system used by the cow.[6]

September 14, 1924, *Boston Daily Globe*

Most farmers are slaves to their animals. They stick in their farms the year around nursing a few cows and horses.[7]

September 14, 1924, *Boston Daily Globe*

The horse is so inefficient, I marvel that he has lasted this long. He eats his head off in the stable 365 days of the year and generates less power for the fuel he consumes than any source of energy save the elephant.[8]

September 14, 1924, *Boston Daily Globe*

We don't need horses. We've got the tractor. We've got the automobile. We don't need cows—we can make synthetic milk. We can make meat substitute out of soybeans and coconuts—you can hardly tell the difference. We don't need sheep. We will be able to make wool out of synthetic things—it'll be better than wool.[9]

Circa 1930–39

The world would be better off without horses. They can see you every day of their lives and still kick you to death.[10]

Circa 1930–39

John Burroughs, Thomas Edison, and Henry Ford cutting down a tree while on their first camping trip in Florida, 1914. Courtesy Florida State Archives, RC09775.

The horse is DONE.[11]

Circa 1930–39

On Agriculture

I think the normal life for a man is to get back on the land. The land is the healthiest way to be.[12]

Circa 1910–14

We shall get more food not by bookkeeping and clerical regulation in the cities but by the use of more and better machinery on the land.[13]

March 25, 1918, *New York Times*

I am a farmer. I want to see every acre of the earth's surface covered with little farms, with happy, contented people living on them.[14]

September 1918, *World's Work*

Nothing could be more inexcusable than the average farmer, his wife and their children, drudging from early morning until late at night.[15]

November 1921, *Review of Reviews*

I have followed many a weary mile behind a plow and I know all the drudgery of it.[16]

Circa 1923

It was life on the farm that drove me into devising ways and means to better transportation.[17]

Circa 1923

I never had any particular love for the farm. It was the mother on the farm I loved.[18]

July 1923, *American Magazine*

To lift farm drudgery off flesh and blood and lay it on steel and motors has been my most constant ambition.[19]

Circa 1923

The soil ought to give us our food and our happiness and it ought not to be our master.[20]

Circa 1923

That is instinctive. We all want to get back to the soil. We all like to camp out. That is primitive and instinctive.[21]

Circa 1923

The most inefficient man in the world is the farmer. No old-fashioned farmer ever made money. One trouble with him is that he does not figure his own time as valuable.[22]

September 14, 1924, *Boston Daily Globe*

Farming in the future is going to be organized on a big scale, just as industry is.[23]

September 14, 1924, *Boston Daily Globe*

There wouldn't be any animals.[24]

Circa 1929, on his ideal farm

On Chemurgy

The fuel of the future is going to come from fruit like that sumach [*sic*] out by the road, or from apples, weeds, sawdust—almost anything.[25]

September 20, 1925, *New York Times*

There is an enormous waste on farms that is needless. There is hardly any product of the soil which cannot be turned into some sort of economic use.[26]

June 20, 1926, *New York Times*

For it is fully within my expectation some day to see the materials for an automobile body grown and manufactured on what we now call a farm.[27]

May 16, 1931, *Saturday Evening Post*

And surely a good papermaking material can be grown as an annual crop and our forests saved for their higher uses.[28]

May 16, 1931, *Saturday Evening Post*

We must harness the surplus of the farm to the surplus of industry. Isn't the soya bean a sign it can be done? Our automobiles are all to be painted with the oil from this humble bean.[29]

Circa April 1933

I think farmers are going to disappear in the course of time. Yes, and factory workers too. Every man will be a farmer some day, and every man will work in a factory or office.[30]

Circa 1940–49

On Village Industries

What I am going to do is to establish plants for manufacturing parts of Ford cars and Fordson tractors in places where they will be within easy reach of farming districts, and provide employment for farmers and their families in winter.[31]

September 1919, *World's Work*

Next year every man with a family who is employed at the plant will be required to have a garden of sufficient size to supply his family with at least part of its Winter vegetables. Those who do not comply with the rule will be discharged.[32]

August 24, 1931, *New York Times*. Ford later denied making the statement.

The man too lazy to work in a garden during his leisure time does not deserve a job.[33]

August 24, 1931, *New York Times*. Ford later denied this statement as well.

With one foot on the land and one foot in industry, America is safe.[34]

Circa 1940–47

Of course the steady desertion of the farm cannot continue forever. Too many people have believed that Santa Claus lives in the city.[35]

Circa 1940s

On Plastics

And don't forget: The motor-car business is just one of the businesses that can find new uses for plastics made from what is grown in the land. There's no end to what can be done with them if we know how![36]

March 1941, *Popular Science*

On Forestry

We do not waste our lumber by letting forest fires burn it up. We keep our woods cleared out. The ordinary logger leaves a pile of debris and after it lies a year it gets dry and makes a good fire. We clean up every stick of wood. Consequently, we have had little fire losses.[37]

October 26, 1923, *New York Times*

On Ecology and Conservation

We don't want to destroy all the growth there is there just because we are going to operate this mill today. Look out for tomorrow, next month, next year.[38]

Circa 1920–30, on lumbering at Iron Mountain

The earth never ceases making what we need and is prepared to fill future needs, of which we have not now the slightest knowledge. If men waste energy, it is lost to them as individuals—but the great reservoir of energy on which all life draws is not exhausted. Therefore, the great word of life is "Use."[39]

June 1928, *World's Work*

On Power and Energy

This is the age of power. Electricity and gasoline are emancipating the human race from the slavery of primitive drudgery.[40]

July 1922, *Popular Science*

On Fuels

I believe alcohol, made from farm waste, will eventually take the place of gasolene [*sic*] and kerosene.[41]

September 1918, *World's Work*

So far as the so-called fuel situation is concerned, we always have had our calamity howlers. We shall have gasoline as long as we need it.[42]

July 1922, *Popular Science*

Every so often we are told that the supply of petroleum can last only a few years. . . . [W]henever a shortage in any commodity develops[,] a new and better substitute will be found for it.[43]

June 1928, *World's Work*

On Coal and Coal Mining

I predict—mind you, this is only a prediction—that in a time not far off, we will not think of using coal for fuel.[44]

November 1921, *Review of Reviews*

On Hydroelectric Power

There is enough water power running to waste to turn every wheel in the world and provide all the light and heat the whole world needs.[45]

September 1918, *World's Work*

Water power is the cheapest, the most efficient, and the least wasteful of all types of power.[46]

Circa 1922–29

18 ⚙ On Family

Henry Ford was the eldest of six children born to a farming family in what is now Dearborn, Michigan. His mother, with whom he was very close, died when he was thirteen. Three years later, he left home to work as a machinist in Detroit. In 1885, Ford developed a friendship with a childhood acquaintance named Clara Bryant. The two were married in 1888.

Clara was devoted to her husband but stood firmly when she disagreed with him. In 1923, she had her name removed from her husband's increasingly controversial *Dearborn Independent*. She told him she wouldn't support him in a run for president and threatened to leave him if he broke up Ford Motor Company instead of negotiating with the United Auto Workers. Ford died a few days short of their sixty-second anniversary.

Their son, Edsel, was born in 1893. Father and son had a complex relationship. Ford turned his company over to Edsel in 1918 but in actuality continued to run it, often undermining his son's authority. Edsel died in 1943 from stomach cancer. Edsel and his wife, Eleanor, had four children: Henry II, Benson, Josephine, and William.

Henry, Clara, and Edsel Ford aboard a ship to Europe. The Ford family journeyed to Ireland in 1912 to trace his roots. From the Collections of the Henry Ford, THF25052.

On Mary Litogot Ford, His Mother

The house was like a watch without a mainspring.[1]

Circa 1916, on his mother's death in 1876

You see that home? That's my mother's home. My father just walked into that place. That belonged to my mother.[2]

Circa 1910–19

She read what was in my mind. . . . It was a way she had. I understand it better now, for I've done it myself many times.[3]

July 1923, *American Magazine*

My mother is in my workshops. She is in my workshops to this extent—it is impossible for me to tolerate disorder or uncleanliness [*sic*].[4]

August 4, 1928, *Milwaukee Sentinel*

On William Ford, His Father

My father was not entirely in sympathy with my bent toward mechanics. He thought that I ought to be a farmer.[5]

Circa 1922

I wish my father could have lived to see what happened.[6]

Circa 1930s

On Clara Ford, His Wife

Clara Dear, you can not imagine what pleasure it gives me to think that i have at last found one so loveing kind and true as you are and i hope we will always have good success.[7]

Love letter sent between 1885 and 1888

I wish she would quit darning my socks. I think I've got enough money to afford new ones.[8]

Circa 1920–29

I often consult with my wife with regard to business affairs because I know her judgment is good, and many times I take her advice. But I am always the one to decide what I shall do.[9]

December 1922, *Hearst's International*

She was *the believer*.[10]

September 1923, *Ladies' Home Journal*

I would not have made it without Clara.[11]

Circa 1930–39

She became frantic about it. She insisted that I sign what she termed a peace agreement. If I did not, she was through. . . . What could I do? I know now she was right. The whole thing was not worth the trouble it would make. I felt her vision and judgment were better than mine. I'm glad that I did see it her way.[12]

Circa 1941. Clara demanded that he sign a contract with the United Auto Workers.

If I were to die and come back in another life, I would want the same wife.[13]

August 16, 1947, *Saturday Evening Post*

On Edsel Ford, His Son

Yes, I have a fine son to carry on. If he keeps on as he is now this company will be in good hands someday.[14]

Circa 1910–19

Why should I want to accumulate a big estate? Why, I have nobody to leave it to.[15]

January 9, 1914, *New York Times*. Ford seemed to have forgotten his son.

My son is a worker.[16]

January 11, 1914, *New York Times*

Edsel, you shut up![17]

Circa 1926, Ford's refusal to consider his son's suggestion for hydraulic brakes

Edsel has his own mind and his own ideas. He knows some things better than I do, and I know some things better than he does.[18]

August 1928, *World's Work*

If there is anything the matter with Edsel's health, he can correct it himself.[19]

Circa 1943, denial of the cancer that would eventually kill his son

I just can't get over it. I've got a lump right here. Clara sits down and cries and gets over it, feels a little better. I just cannot do it. I just have a lump here, and there is nothing I can do about it.[20]

Circa May 1943, on the death of Edsel

That's what I wanted him to do—get mad.[21]

Circa 1943–47, reflection upon his treatment of his son before his death. Henry wanted Edsel to stand up to him.

On His Grandchildren

Let them alone. They run wild when they're with me because the rest of the time they're cooped up like caged lions. They are so penned in at home by bodyguards that when they are with me I want to let them loose.[22]

Circa 1920–29

I can replace factories but not grandchildren.[23]

Circa 1930–39. A Detroit crime wave and fears of kidnapping induced Ford to increase security for his family.

19 ⚙ On Himself

Henry Ford seldom discussed his own achievements. Given his belief that hard work resulted in success, it may have been a result of modesty, real or false. When acknowledging his accomplishments, he ascribed them to divine guidance rather than his own hard work. His success seemed to be preordained. "I don't think that there was any chance of failure."[1]

I always knew I would get what I went after. I don't recall having any very great doubts or fears.[2]

Circa 1917

Why, everything I ever did selfishly in my life has come back like a boomerang and hurt me more than it hurt any one else, and the same way with everything I have done to help others. It helps me in the end every time.[3]

Circa 1917

You know me too well. Hereafter, I am going to see to it that no man comes to know me so intimately.[4]

Circa 1910–19, said following the departure of a trusted employee, possibly Harold Wills

Portrait of Henry Ford. Courtesy of the Library of Congress, LC-USZ62-111360.

I guess I'm the only businessman in America who can afford to say what he thinks. I don't care what I say.[5]

November 1916, *Current Opinion*

I don't drink or smoke—tho [*sic*] I have had curiosity enough to taste everything—but that don't mean that I'm right. If it doesn't hurt you, why should you quit? That's all. Only I believe in moderation. I don't want to stop anything, and I don't want to suppress anything.[6]

November 1916, *Current Opinion*. Ford abhorred smoking and drinking and fired employees who did either in his factories.

I'll admit I'm an "ignorant idealist!"[7]

July 17, 1919, *New York Tribune*, said at trial during his libel suit against the *Chicago Tribune*, in reference to his pre–World War I peace campaign

I have never pretended to be a writer or an editor, but I can talk with plain Americans in a way that we can understand each other.[8]

Circa 1919, from the first issue of his *Dearborn Independent*

I could not possibly do the same thing day in and day out.[9]

Circa 1923. Ford freely admitted he would not like assembly-line work.

I never forget appointments. It is one of the first principles of business.[10]

October 29, 1922, *New York Times*

I curry favor with no man.[11]

October 29, 1922, *New York Times*

I am more interested in people than I am in profits.[12]

May 9, 1923, *Outlook*

I am an optimist.[13]

June 10, 1923, *New York Times*

I am in a peculiar position. No one can give me anything. There is little I want that I cannot have. But I do not want many of the things money can buy. I want to live a life, to make the world a little better for having lived in it.[14]

September 1923, *Current Opinion*

You talk about me too much. Leave that out. Every time you come across an "I" cross it out. Always say "we."[15]

Circa 1923, comment to a reporter

I'm too fidgety. I couldn't sit still for that long. I'd have to get out and walk around.[16]

December 5, 1927, *New York Times*, on why he wouldn't attend the 1928 Republican Convention

I knew that if I worked hard enough I would come out. I don't think that there was any chance of failure.[17]

Circa 1928

My particular job, this time on earth, is to give the world the very best car I can make at the lowest possible price.[18]

August 28, 1929, *New York Times*

That's right. Makes me feel spunky. I put it on to match my temper.[19]

Circa 1930–39, on wearing red ties when he was angry

There was no way for me to escape doing what I did. I had an idea, and it was impossible to get away from it; it just had to be born. That is why I never take credit for anything I have done—I had to do it.[20]

January 12, 1926, *New York Times*

Every one has his own guiding compass. But I feel that for myself, if I had not gone where I was pushed, I would have done very little.[21]

January 12, 1926, *New York Times*

I'm not a business man. I never have been one. I've just been a very lucky man. I had what the people wanted—and Mrs. Ford.[22]

Circa 1941

I don't care what anybody says, so long as they talk about Ford.[23]

Date unknown

It is not necessary to expose your inner self to anyone.[24]

Date unknown

I've answered questions before they were asked; I've seen people approaching me and known before they reached me what they were going to propose.[25]

Date unknown, on his belief that he had precognition

I don't do so much, I just go around lighting fires under other people.[26]

Date unknown, on his management style

I wonder whether any of mine will do that at my funeral. Probably not.[27]

Circa 1938, on Harvey Firestone's employees weeping at his funeral

On His Fame

You know, I think I ought to get a pair of whiskers. Everybody seems to spot me.[28]

Circa 1910–19

I am not seeking notoriety; I'm just doing what I think is right.[29]

January 11, 1914, *New York Times*

We were pestered to death![30]

Circa 1920–29

Most of us will never attain fame, and that is a pity, because then we shall never have the opportunity to realize how well off we were without it.[31]

October 1930, *Harper's Magazine*

You're not appreciated until you're dead, and then they get it all wrong on why you should be appreciated.[32]

Circa 1940–47

20 ⚙ On Miscellaneous Topics

On Aesthetics and Design

Our clothing, our food, our household furnishings—all could be much simpler than they now are and at the same time be better looking.[1]

Circa 1923

The design is what counts. Everything in this world, to be made rightly, had to follow a design, and time spent in getting a thing right is never wasted.[2]

Circa 1926

Bizarre Statements

I'm not mentioning the Klan or the Masons or the Knights of Columbus, but I'm including all of them. A majority of the organizations thriving in the United States today are breeding spots [f]or trouble that easily may enlarge into another war.[3]

October 31, 1925, *New York Times*. Ford would later become a Fourth Degree Mason.

Henry Ford lacing his boots, circa 1919. From the Collections of the Henry Ford, THF3975.

The globe has been inhabited by intelligent people millions of times; and very ancient people, I believe were highly developed in the arts and sciences. I believe they had all or most of the things which we think are the creations of modern progress and some things that we haven't heard of. I am sure they had the automobile, the radio, the airplane—everything we have, or its equivalent, and perhaps many things that we have yet to discover.[4]

January 1928, *McClure's Magazine*. Ford later denied making the statement.

Please make every effort to find Sandy.[5]

June 5, 1939, *Life*. Telegram sent by Ford when Sandy, Annie's dog, was lost in the *Little Orphan Annie* comic strip.

On Change

People are always talking about standardization, and I don't like the word. There's no such thing. . . . The only constant thing in the world is change.[6]
November 1921, *Review of Reviews*

You've got to move fast to keep up with this old world. You've got to hold on tight or you'll find yourself in the discard. You've got to keep moving all the time.[7]
Circa 1923

Stability is a dead fish floating downstream. The only kind of stability we know in this country is change.[8]
Circa 1926–29

Be ready to revise any system, scrap any method, abandon any theory, if the success of the job requires it.[9]
September 10, 1927, *Dearborn Independent*

Change may be good or bad, but it certainly means something different.[10]
July 1933, *Good Housekeeping*

Change is the law of life.[11]
February 1936, *American Magazine*

On Cleanliness

The cleanliness of a man's machine also—although cleaning a machine is no part of his duty—is usually an indication of his intelligence.[12]
Circa 1923

One cannot have morale without cleanliness. We tolerate makeshift cleanliness no more than makeshift methods.[13]
Circa 1923

An inefficient process is almost invariably a "dirty" one. All waste is a kind of dirt.[14]

August 1929, *American Magazine*

I want my shops to be as clean as my mother's kitchen.[15]

January 1947, *Rotarian*

On Criticism

The more criticism the better. By criticism I get my education.[16]

Circa October 1915

My wife doesn't like the criticism to which I have been subjected. My son holds a different view and doesn't mind it. I like it; I hope it won't stop. You know the best fertilizer in the world is weeds.[17]

January 3, 1916, *New York Times*

On Death

As for myself, I shall keep on working to the last of my task. When that is finished I shall pass on. I shall not ask for a year or a month or a week or a single day in which to sit down and do nothing here.[18]

July 1923, *American Magazine*

I don't know anything about the end of the road—we are a long way from any ending. But we shall get what we deserve. We all get what we deserve.[19]

September 3, 1928, *Time*

On Dishonesty

Better not try to cheat either, for dishonesty is a dry-rot that creeps in everywhere.[20]

Circa 1922

Swindlers are never clever. Their constant contact with an inferior form of mind in their victims robs them of the opportunity to become clever.[21]

December 19, 1925, *Dearborn Independent*

The man who permits himself to be cheated is just as bad as the man who cheats him.[22]

January 12, 1936, *New York Times*

On Equality

Most certainly all men are not equal, and any democratic conception which strives to make men equal is only an effort to block progress.[23]

Circa 1923

On Evil

Bankers, munitions makers, alcoholic drink, Kings and their henchmen, and school books lay at the root of the world's evils.[24]

July 18, 1919, *New York World*

The people have the evils they deserve, no more, no less.[25]

Circa 1922

What we call evil is simply ignorance bumping its head in the dark.[26]

January 1930, *Theosophist*

On Failure

We won't fail. We can't fail. We'll either succeed or I'll die in the attempt.[27]

Circa 1922

Failure is only the opportunity more intelligently to begin again. There is no disgrace in honest failure; there is disgrace in fearing to fail.[28]

Circa 1923

If you keep on recording all of your failures you will shortly have a list showing that there is nothing left for you to try.[29]

Circa 1923

On Fear

One who fears the future, who fears failure, limits his activities.[30]

Circa 1923

Most of the bars we beat against are in ourselves—*we put them there, and we can take them down.*[31]

February 1941, *American Magazine*

On Freedom

Freedom is the right to work a decent length of time and to get a decent living doing so; to be able to arrange the little personal details of one's own life. . . . The minor forms of Freedom lubricate the everyday life of all of us.[32]

Circa 1923

On Friends and Friendship

People always think better, work better, see more clearly when they are in harmony with the people whom they know.[33]

Circa 1922

And I have come to the conclusion that the best friend one has is the man who tells him the truth.[34]

Circa 1923, referring to Rev. Samuel Marquis. Years later when Marquis's *Henry Ford: An Interpretation*, was released, Ford found his truth so unpleasant that his employees destroyed copies of the book.

Your best friend is the one who can bring out the best that is in you.[35]

Circa 1923

On Fools

There are two fools in this world. One is the millionaire who thinks that by hoarding money he can somehow accumulate real power, and the other is the penniless reformer who thinks that if only he can take the money from one class and give it to another, all the world's ills will be cured.[36]

Circa 1923

On the Future

Every man's future rests solely with himself.[37]

Circa 1923

Yet I believe the time will come when man—in some one of his mental stages or planes of consciousness, if you wish to call it that—will know what is going on in other planets, perhaps be able to visit them. When one looks back at the distance we have traveled mentally, in even the last fifty years, great things may be possible within the next century.[38]

Circa 1928

I never prophesy.[39]

Circa 1928

The man of tomorrow can have luxuries unknown today, by reason of the machine and what the machine can do for him.[40]

May 24, 1931, *New York Times*

The promise of the future makes the present seem drab.[41]

September 13, 1931, *New York Times*

Electricity will do the housework. Not only for the rich but for nearly every one.[42]

July 1933, *Good Housekeeping*

Of course, progress has acquired momentum now, and changes will be more numerous and rapid in the future.[43]

January 12, 1936, *New York Times*

On Genius

The genius walks into his success. The rest of us must work for ours.[44]

Circa 1922

On Good

Good grows and multiplies of itself and crowds wrong to the corners; it is wrong that struggles and fights; the good does not have to.[45]

Circa 1922

On the Grand Cross of the German Eagle Award

Why, I never had my picture taken with that medal. That was faked.[46]

Circa August 1930, denying that he posed for a photo accepting the Grand Cross of the German Eagle, given as a birthday present from Adolph Hitler[47]

Those who know me for many years know that anything that breeds hate is repulsive to me.[48]

Circa 1939, his alleged disavowal of the award

On Happiness

[T]hat's what it is—what the modern family needs to learn—the art of being happy with each other.[49]

July 14, 1923, *Literary Digest*

The best day I ever had in my life.[50]

Circa 1923, his regular response to his wife's question, "Well, Henry, what kind of a day did you have to-day?"

Happiness is on the road. When you get there, when you get to the top, you will find the top has a very sharp point.[51]

May 11, 1926, *Boston Daily Globe*

[H]appiness in life is usually found by the man who is looking for something else.[52]

December 17, 1929, *New York Times*

On Haste

People are in too much of a hurry. They want to succeed, to accumulate, to get quick returns, so that they can get away and play. They work hard, in order to be able to quit working.[53]

November 1921, *Review of Reviews*

Haste is a great maker of discouragement.[54]

April 8, 1947, *Toledo (Ohio) Blade*

On the Home

I don't know whether mothers of to-day are different, but it seems to me that a lot of people don't make good use of their homes as they should. When they want a good time they go down-town, or to the club, or some other place to get it. That's all a mistake. The best times I have now I have at home with the family.[55]

July 14, 1923, *Literary Digest*

What is a home anyhow? Not just four walls closing you in from the world. A home is the place where you get your finest experience. It is the place where you grow, where you do the things that give you strength and inspiration to go on with your work.[56]

September 1923, *Ladies' Home Journal*

Our young women are going to keep house in a manner different from that of their mothers. But so did their mothers before them.[57]

Circa 1928

On Honesty

Telling the truth pays. You'll find out. The minute you let anybody tell you what to say, you're a goner.[58]

August 21, 1922, *New York Times*

One ounce of fair dealing is worth a ton of fair speeches.[59]

Circa 1922

It is much easier to make money honestly than to make it dishonestly.[60]

July 11, 1926, *New York Times*

On Human Rights

Every inalienable right we now possess was once a "class privilege."[61]

Circa 1922

[I]t is well to remember that there are instances where the privilege of the few is really a prophecy of the coming rights of the many.[62]

Circa 1922

On Ideas

What do I mean by a good idea? I mean an idea that will work out for the best interests of every one—an idea for something that will benefit the world. That's the kind of idea the world wants.[63]

Circa 1917

Well, I can pick mechanics, and I can pick businessmen. When it comes to ideas I haven't had much experience. But I'm learning.[64]

November 1916, *Current Opinion*

Get ideas. The men who command the largest salaries in the industrial life of the world today are the men who have ideas and who work them out to success.[65]

January 25, 1919, *New York Times*

Ideas have a hard time being born, and restlessness is part of the general operation.[66]

Circa 1922

It is better to be skeptical of all new ideas and to insist upon being shown rather than to rush around in a continuous brainstorm after every new idea.[67]

Circa 1923

If an idea seems good or seems to have possibilities, I believe in doing whatever is necessary to test the idea from every angle.[68]

Circa 1923

There is only one thing stronger than armies and that is an idea whose time has come.[69]

Circa 1920–29

On Idleness and Laziness

Idleness warps the mind.[70]

Circa 1922

Any man who tells you that men prefer the dog's life loafing to the real life of going after something and getting it done, does not know men.[71]

Circa 1928

Most of the world's mischief is born of idleness.[72]

November 21, 1927, *New York Times*

The unhappiest man on earth is the one who has nothing to do.[73]

May 28, 1944, *Detroit Free Press*

On Knowledge

The basis of all knowledge is a knowledge of how far one is behind—not necessarily behind others, but how far his efforts fall short of the ideal.[74]

March 31, 1907, *Boston Daily Globe*

Why should I clutter my mind with general information when I have men around me who can supply any knowledge I need?[75]

Circa 1920–29

The less you know the more quickly you can learn.[76]

Circa 1917

You must know all there is to know of your particular field, and keep on the alert for new knowledge. The least difference in knowledge between you and another man may spell his success and your failure. Guessing does not go. Trusting luck is folly. Going blind is taking a chance that may prove disastrous. You must KNOW.[77]

Circa 1922

The only reason why every man does not know everything that the human mind has ever learned is that no one has ever found it worth while to know that much.[78]

Circa 1923

And yet with all our progress we know very little. We know nothing or comparatively nothing about the biggest thing or the smallest thing—little about the universe around us, and little about the atom.[79]

Circa 1928

Knowledge doesn't amount to any thing.[80]

June 1935, *Time*

A man learns something even by being hanged.[81]

March 17, 1941, *Time*

On the Ku Klux Klan

It is the victim of a mass of lying propaganda and is therefore looked upon with disfavor in many quarters. But if the truth were known about it, it would be looked upon as a patriotic body, concerned with nothing but future development of the country in which it was born and the preservation of the supremacy of the true American in his own land.[82]

August 27, 1924, *New York Times*. Ford later denied making the statement.

On Leadership

I suppose executive ability is born to you. It has to come through in its own way. Though there is less difference between men than we imagine. What one can do, another may.[83]

April 1914, *Everybody's Magazine*

That's the only way to get anywhere—one man rule.[84]

Circa 1910s

The restless boy, the one who wants to know why things are as they are, and why they can't be done better, shows signs of possible leadership. At times he may be a nuisance. But no boy ever became a leader without making himself a nuisance to somebody—at some time.[85]

August 1929, *American Magazine*

What is a leader, anyhow? It is a man who visualizes what the people want and goes ahead and produces it.[86]

October 3, 1930, *New York Times*

On Life

What are we here on earth for? Only to get experience. A man is born when he wants to, and dies when he wants to and the only time he's in trouble is when he isn't getting experience.[87]

October 1916, *Metropolitan Magazine*

Life, as I see it, is not a location but a journey.[88]

Circa 1923

Everything is in flux, and was meant to be. Life flows.[89]

Circa 1923

Life is a going concern. It is going somewhere. It never stagnates.[90]
February 1936, *American Magazine*

On Mistakes

Maybe you don't think your judgment is good, but offer it anyhow. One mistake may sharpen your wits.[91]
Circa January 1917

I never made a mistake in my life. Never! And neither did you ever make a mistake—or anybody else.[92]
January 7, 1928, *Literary Digest*

Mistakes are a source of experience; and it is the essence of experience that we call wisdom.[93]
Circa 1928

It isn't getting lost that usually does the damage, it's losing our heads.[94]
July 1933, *Good Housekeeping*

Each mistake carries with it an ache of some sort.[95]
Circa 1930s

Don't find fault; find a remedy; anybody can complain.[96]
Circa 1930s

On Praise

We are such simple creatures that we imagine the race is run the moment the cheers are heard.[97]
Circa 1922

All men like praise. If a man says that he doesn't, he should examine himself again.[98]

Circa 1922

Make your program so long and so hard that the people who praise you will always seem to you to be talking about something very trivial in comparison with what you are really trying to do.[99]

Circa 1922

You never want to praise a man, because that's the way to spoil him.[100]

Date unknown

On Pride

A little observation will show that a man given to pride is usually proud of the wrong thing.[101]

September 10, 1927, *Dearborn Independent*

On Problems, Challenges, and Discouragement

Most people spend more time and energy going around problems than in trying to solve them.[102]

Circa 1928

I was never discouraged in my life. Discouragement comes from fear and haste.[103]

April 8, 1947, *Toledo (Ohio) Blade*

On Progress

The whole progress of the world has been made by men who went to work and used their impractical theories.[104]

Circa 1917

Progress is not made by pulling off a series of stunts. Each step has to be regulated. A man cannot expect progress without thinking.[105]

Circa 1923

Progress is geared to every man's gait. Being dragged along is where the strain comes in. Keeping step is keeping fit.[106]

Circa 1924

There is nothing that cannot be improved upon.[107]

October 19, 1930, *New York Times*

No *good* thing is ever rendered obsolete by progress.[108]

June 1936, *Rotarian*

On Property

When a few people own most of the land there cannot be real liberty. . . . What we must do is to give everyone a chance to own his own piece of land and teach him how to live on it.[109]

September 1918, *World's Work*

I do not believe any one should be permitted to hold land out of use, and nobody should keep for himself more land than he can cultivate to the limit of profitable productiveness.[110]

September 1918, *World's Work*

Demagogues talked a long time about "putting property rights above human rights," but it is very noticeable that in Russia when they abolished property rights, they abolished human rights also. When you do not respect the things that a man has gathered around him by his own labor for the use of his family, you don't respect his right to life.[111]

Circa 1922

On Public Speaking

You say it for me.[112]

November 26, 1915, terrified response when asked to address an audience at the Belasco Theatre

I certainly would not make a public speech to get the nomination or to be elected.[113]

September 1918, *World's Work*, response to the possibility that he might run for U.S. senator

This is the first speech I ever made in my life. I am glad to be here and I am glad to see you children all so clean and healthy. That remark will cause some of my party to laugh, but I will explain it later. I thank you.[114]

Circa November 1926, entire speech to schoolchildren in Gatlinburg, Tennessee

You know I don't make speeches; I make cars.[115]

December 8, 1933, *New York Times*

On Success

There is one principle which a man must follow if he wishes to succeed, and that is to understand human nature.[116]

Circa 1919

Success is the enemy.[117]

Circa 1922

More men are failures on account of success, than on account of failure.[118]

Circa 1922

The man who thinks he has done something, hasn't many more things to do.[119]

Circa 1922

If success comes you will have to work twice as hard to keep on top of it; once it gets on top of you, then success becomes your failure.[120]

Circa 1922

We want to write the word "success" too soon. It should be kept for the epitaph.[121]

Circa 1922

But success does not come by imitation. An imitation may be quite successful in its own way, but imitation can never be success.[122]

Circa 1922

The road to Success is hard, and often the feet bleed and the heart nearly fails. People only see the end of it, and even the end is not all sunshine.[123]

Circa 1922

The best road to the white collar is through blue-jeans and practical brains.[124]

Circa 1924

The world is full of greatness that we never hear of.[125]

Circa 1928

The successful man is not only ready to handle anything that comes up; he is ready for it before it comes up.[126]

January 12, 1936, *New York Times*

On Thinking and Intelligence

Right thinking is the first step toward right doing.[127]

Circa January 1917

Thinking which does not connect with constructive action becomes a disease; the man who has it sees crooked; his views are lopsided.[128]

Circa 1922

In fact, to some types of mind thought is absolutely appalling. To them the ideal job is one where the creative instinct need not be expressed. . . . [A]bove all, he wants a job in which he does not have to think.[129]

Circa 1923

There is a certain amount of mental inertia to be overcome in the promotion of any new thing.[130]

Circa 1928

But the job of thinking is a real one—probably the hardest work there is to do. Yet I believe that all the world's secrets are open to thinkers, and that whenever a problem comes to us, it can always be solved.[131]

Circa 1928

It doesn't matter that all do not think alike—to think is the thing.[132]

November 8, 1931, *New York Times*

[T]here never can be any substitute for thinking. We are going to depend more and more upon our heads and less and less upon our muscles.[133]

July 1933, *Good Housekeeping*

The human mind is a channel through which things-to-be are coming into the realm of things that are.[134]

Date unknown

On Thrift

Society lives by circulation, and not by congestion.[135]

Circa 1923, on why it's better to spend than save.

The thrift of the future is not penny saving, but time saving.[136]

July 1933, *Good Housekeeping*

On Waste

What we call waste is only surplus, and surplus is only the starting point of new uses.[137]

May 29, 1930, *New York Times*

Time waste differs from material waste in that there can be no salvage.[138]

Date unknown

On Weather

Well, you can't change the weather, so you better change your attitude toward it.[139]

Circa 1930–39

On Women's Clothing

I think that dress reform for women—which seems to mean ugly clothes—must always originate with plain women who want to make everyone else look plain.[140]

Circa 1923

You ladies and girls are showing very poor taste and worse judgment in coming into the town garbed as you are, without skirts or dresses. I do not want to sign my name for you and prefer not to look at you. I resent your idea of dress.[141]

September 3, 1923, *Time*, on women and girls wearing overalls

On Wrongs

Nobody ought to assume for a moment that because something is wrong it has got to stay wrong.[142]

Circa 1922

The only power any wrong can exert over us is to make us believe that it is here to stay. Expose its transient character and its sting is drawn.[143]

Circa 1922

21 ⚙ Henry Ford on Others

William Jennings Bryan (1860–1925), Lawyer and Presidential Candidate

I forgot William Jennings Bryan twenty years ago.[1]

January 16, 1920, *New York Times*, response to Bryan's run for president

John Burroughs (1839–1921), Naturalist

There was something very simple about him and yet with it all there was a thoroughness of investigation and hardihood of endurance that gave him rank as a natural man. . . . For him the deserted wilderness was more alive than the populous cities. That was the main characteristic of Mr. Burroughs—he was alive and his eyes were open.[2]

March 30, 1921, *New York Times*

[T]o know John Burroughs and to sit in his company was one of the privileges of life.[3]

April 2, 1921, *New York Times*

George Washington Carver (1864–1943), Scientist

Dr. Carver had the brain of a scientist and the heart of a saint.[4]
Circa January 1943

I have never known a man who knew so much about everything.[5]
February 1943, *Fortune*

James Couzens (1872–1936), Ford Motor Company Associate and U.S. Senator

Couzens is just the type of man needed in the Senate, not only by Michigan but by the whole country.[6]
December 3, 1922, *New York Times*, endorsement of Couzens's senatorial bid

Jim was trying to make a sucker out of me.[7]
February 27, 1933, *Time*, response to a request that Couzens and Ford endorse a note as collateral to bail out a troubled bank

Thomas Alva Edison (1847–1931), Inventor

In my opinion Edison to-day is the top man of the world. He is the man who has done most for it.[8]
January 11, 1914, *New York Times*

I have found Mr. Edison an inspiration. He is, I believe, the happiest man in the world.[9]
March 7, 1929, *New York Times*

Harvey Firestone (1868–1938), Rubber Manufacturer

He was a fine man. During all those years we did business, I knew I could trust his word all the way. And I think he felt he could trust mine.[10]
Circa 1930–39

Mohandas Karamchand Gandhi (1869–1948), Indian Political and Spiritual Leader

I admire your life and message. You are one of the greatest men the world has ever known. May God help and guide your lofty work.[11]

Circa 1940–47, letter to Gandhi

Adolph Hitler (1889–1945), German Dictator

I have never met Hitler. I have never contributed a cent directly, or in any other way to any anti-Semitic activity anywhere.[12]

Circa December 1933

When you see the Fuhrer after your return, tell him that I admire him and I am looking forward to meeting him at the coming party rally in Nuremberg.[13]

Circa 1938. There is no record that Ford ever met Hitler.

You know, he's following my example of producing a car for the millions. He got his engineers to come up with a cheap "people's car"—Volkswagen. I think I just may have his respect, the door may be open.[14]

Circa 1940

Well, by God, we're through with him. He's just power-drunk, like all the rest of them.[15]

Circa 1940, following Hitler's conquests beyond the Polish Corridor

Herbert Hoover (1874–1964), American President

I think of him as a human-hearted, honest-minded, hard-working man.[16]

October 20, 1932, *New York Times*

Henry Ford and Charles Lindbergh. Courtesy of Wayne State University Virtual Motor City Collection, 1485.

William S. Knudsen (1879–1948), Ford Motor Company Executive

I let him go not because he wasn't good, but because he was too good—for me.[17]

Circa 1921, on Knudsen's resignation from the Ford Motor Company

Charles Lindbergh (1902–1974), American Aviator

Men of Lindbergh's stamp have set a new standard, or have revealed to the world the real American standard.[18]

Circa 1928

William Holmes McGuffey (1800–1873), American Educator

He was a great American. The McGuffey Readers taught industry and morality to the youth of America.[19]

Date unknown

Truman Handy Newberry (1864–1945), Senator Who Defeated Ford in His 1919 Senatorial Bid

I have known Mr. Newberry and all his people for many years and I am very sorry for him and them. The big interests have simply victimized him.[20]

December 6, 1919, New York Times

Franklin D. Roosevelt (1882–1945), American President

You never heard me say anything against him, did you? What's the use, what's the use? He's like all the rest of us, trying to do the best he can. Don't you think so? . . . People are looking for a leader. They ought to be their own leaders, but they're looking for a leader. And they've got a leader who is putting something over on them, and they deserve it.[21]

May 9, 1938, *Time*. Ford did not care for Roosevelt's programs and policies.

Theodore Roosevelt (1858–1919), American President

I consider Roosevelt so antiquated that the "ex" [president] business does not mean anything. I consider him just an ordinary citizen because he does not keep up with the times.[22]

May 16, 1916, *New York Times*

Rosika Schwimmer (1877–1948), Hungarian-born Pacifist

She has more brains than all the others on the peace ship put together.[23]

Circa 1914

It is not true that Mme. Schwimmer inspired our peace trip.[24]

February 7, 1916, *Boston Daily Globe*. Ford tried to distance himself from Schwimmer after the Peace Ship expedition.

Woodrow Wilson (1856–1924), American President

He's a small man.[25]

Circa 1915, following Wilson's tepid response to his Peace Ship plans

It is an act of Providence that he is our President today.[26]

November 18, 1917, *Boston Daily Globe*

22 ⚙ Others on Henry Ford

Fred L. Black (1891–1971), Ford Employee

We used to say around Dearborn, that if Henry Ford saw three blackbirds in the morning, all the birds were black that day.[1]

Circa 1920–29, on Ford's habit of jumping to conclusions

Arthur Brisbane (1864–1936), Newspaper Editor and Columnist

[Ford is] a typical specimen of the anti-cultural American.[2]

May 12, 1930, *Time*

Luther Burbank (1849–1926), American Botanist

Henry Ford is a creative genius in his way. He has made something new and something that the common people can afford and enjoy.[3]

Circa 1910–19

John Burroughs (1937–1921), American Naturalist

Mr. Ford's heart is bigger than his head.[4]
Circa 1915, regarding Ford's Peace Ship

As tender as a woman, he is much more tolerant. He looks like a poet and conducts his life like a philosopher. No poet ever expressed himself through his work more completely than Mr. Ford has expressed himself through his car and his tractor engine. They typify him—not imposing, nor complex, less expressive of mass than of simplicity, adaptability and universal service, they typify the combination of powers and qualities which makes him a beneficent, a likeable and unique personality. Those who meet him are invariably drawn to him. He is a national figure, and the crowds that flock around the car in which he is riding are not paying their homage merely to a successful car builder or business man, but to a beneficent human force.[5]
December 1921, *Current Opinion*

W. J. Cameron, (1879–1955), Editor of *Dearborn Independent*

Mr. Ford had a twenty-five track mind and there were trains going out and coming in on all tracks at all times.[6]
Date unknown

Eddie Cantor (1892–1964), American Actor, Singer, Songwriter

Mr. Henry Ford, in my opinion, is a damned fool for permitting the world's greatest gangster to give him this citation. Doesn't he realize that the German papers, reporting the citation, said all Americans were behind Naziism [*sic*]? Whose side is Mr. Ford on?[7]
August 15, 1938, *Time*, reaction to Ford's acceptance of the Grand Cross of the German Eagle from Adolph Hitler

Charlie Chaplin (1889–1977), English Actor

He is getting all the business of the country because he is fair. He gives value received for his merchandise, and on the other hand he considers his workers, pays them a fair wage and has made profit sharing absolutely practicable.[8]

September 18, 1921, *New York Times*

Rev. Charles E. Coughlin (1891–1979), Priest and Radio Broadcaster

[Ford is] the greatest force in the movement to internationalize labor throughout the world.[9]

August 4, 1930, *Time*

Chicago Tribune

If we had a Senate full of Henry Fords the best thing the people of the United States could do would be to put out to sea in lifeboats.[10]

August 25, 1918, *Chicago Tribune*

The election of Mr. Ford . . . would mark the beginning of a rapid degeneration in our government. . . . What makes him impossible as a candidate . . . is that he lacks any sense of his limitations. . . . If a man is both ignorant and ignorant of his ignorance he is not one to put in any place of responsibility.[11]

June 19, 1923, *Chicago Tribune*

James Couzens (1872–1936), Senator and Ford Motor Company Associate

I love him as much as it is possible for one man to love another. Yet . . . [i]t comes with poor taste for a man so politically ambitious. He has never gotten over his defeat as a candidate for the United

States Senator in Michigan. . . . Ford wants to be President. His failure to withdraw his name from the Nebraska primary proves that. Why does he refrain from announcing his candidacy? Because he is afraid. He realizes that it would prove just as great a fiasco as his peace ship.

. . . How can a man over 60 years old, who has done nothing except make motors, who has no training, no experience, aspire to such an office? It is ridiculous. . . . I say this not only because I want to save Mr. Ford from the greatest humiliation that could befall him, but I want equally to save the United States from the humiliation it would suffer.[12]

November 1, 1923, *New York Times*

John Cote Dahlinger (1923–1984), likely Ford's illegitimate son

And I want to say a few words in praise of Mr. Ford's treatment of me. Given the mores of the early '20s, the years when I was growing up, he did the right thing. I'm sure he made it much easier for Mother and me. It was relatively scandal-free; not whisper-filled, perhaps, but scandal-free, at least as far as the newspapers were concerned.

He might not have made waves by publicly acknowledging me, but at least he didn't sweep me under the rug. He made a friend of me. For this I salute him.[13]

Circa 1977

Josephus Daniels (1862–1948), Secretary of the U.S. Navy

In war [Ford] knows how to produce weapons to win peace, and in the problems to be settled after the war his practical judgment as Senator would be of the highest value.[14]

October 25, 1918, *New York Times*

Eugene V. Debs (1855–1926), Union Leader and Socialist

Henry Ford has taken thieves, pickpockets, prostitutes, burglars, dope-fiends, murderers, both male and female, who were supposed to be hopeless degenerates and has made men and women of them.[15]

Circa February 4, 1916, on Ford's willingness to hire ex-convicts

I can think of no man less fitted for the Presidency than Mr. Ford.[16]

November 5, 1923, *Time*

John Dillinger (1903–1934), Bank Robber

I want to thank you for making an excellent car. If I am ever captured it will have to be someone in another Ford.[17]

Circa 1930–34

John F. Dodge (1864–1920), Automaker

I am tired of being carried around in Henry Ford's vest pocket.[18]

Circa 1900–1910. Dodge resigned as vice president and director at Ford Motor Company and established his own company.

Mina Miller Edison (1865–1947), Wife of Inventor Thomas Edison

Dear me, I do wish he would keep out of our backyard![19]

Circa late 1929, reaction to Ford's acquisition of Edison's Florida electrical laboratory

Thomas Alva Edison (1847–1931), Inventor

That's it, young man. You are on the right line. Don't let anybody throw you off.[20]

Circa 1896, encouraging Ford, early in his career, to continue with his gasoline engine

Henry Ford, Thomas Edison, and Harvey Firestone. The men took frequent camping trips during the 1920s. It offered them time together, away from responsibilities and the glare of the public spotlight. Courtesy of the Thomas Edison National Historic Park, 14.475.46.

What do you want to do that for? You can't speak. You wouldn't say a damned word. You'd be mum.[21]

Circa 1920–29, reaction to Ford's interest in the presidency

I would not vote for him for President, but as a director of manufacturing or industrial enterprises I'd vote for him—twice.[22]

Circa 1923

Ford's foresight was so long it sagged in the middle.[23]

Circa 1920–29

As to Henry Ford, words are inadequate to express my feelings. I can only say to you that, in the fullest and richest meaning of the term—he is my friend.[24]

Circa October 1929

Harvey Firestone (1868–1938), Rubber Manufacturer

No one who does business with Mr. Ford ever gets a chance to rest.[25]

Circa 1910–19

Benson Ford (1919–1978), Ford's Grandson

The trouble my father had with my grandfather arose from a basic difference. . . . My father believed in team play, and my grandfather wanted to run a one-man show.[26]

Circa 1950–59

Clara Ford (1866–1947), Wife of Henry Ford

If Henry really went to the White House to live there, he would have to go without me.[27]

April 10, 1923, *Boston Daily Globe*, reaction to her husband's political aspirations

Since you got him into it, you can just get him out of it. I hate the idea of the name Ford being dragged down into the gutters of political filth! My name is Ford and I'm proud of it! If Mr. Ford wants to go to Washington, he can go, but I'll go to England![28]

Circa 1923–29

It wasn't [love at first sight], for me; he made absolutely no impression on me at the time.[29]

September 1923, *Ladies' Home Journal*

I always knew Mr. Ford would come out right in the end. And for-bearance—there were times when I couldn't understand what Mr. Ford was doing. The hardest was at the time of the Peace Ship.[30]

September 1923, *Ladies' Home Journal*

Edsel Ford (1893–1943), Son of Henry Ford

Well, after all, my father built this business. It's his business.[31]

Circa 1930–39. Despite the fact he was president of the Ford Motor Company, Edsel generally deferred to his father.

Father is in a terrible state of mind.[32]

Circa 1940–43. Ford experienced a mental decline during his late seventies and early eighties.

Henry Ford II (1917–1987), Ford's Grandson

My grandfather killed my father in my mind. I know he died of cancer—but it was because of what my grandfather did to him.[33]

Date unknown

William Ford (1826–1905), Ford's Father

Oh, Henry ain't much of a farmer. He's more of a tinkerer.[34]

Date unknown

Henry worries me. He doesn't seem to settle down and I don't know what's going to become of him.[35]

Date unknown. William died in 1907, before his son had achieved great success.

Philip Fox (1897–1965), Wisconsin Governor

He has his feet in 1937 and his head in 1837.[36]

September 6, 1937, *Time,* labor-friendly Fox criticizing Ford's unwillingness to allow unions

Mohandas Karamchand Gandhi (1869–1948), Indian Political and Spiritual Leader

I believe there is a tremendous fallacy behind Mr. Ford's ideas. . . . This mass production is possible only because these nations are able to exploit the so-called weaker or unorganized races of the world.[37]

November 8, 1931, *New York Times*

Cardinal Gibbons (1834–1932), Archbishop of Baltimore, Maryland

Mr. Ford impressed me as a very modest gentleman. I had, perhaps, expected to find a more aggressive type. . . . I could not but admire his roseate view of the future.[38]

November 28, 1915, *New York Times*

Edgar A. Guest (1881–1959), American Poet

His was a sensitive heart . . . an understanding mind. . . . He had sympathy and pity for the woes of others.[39]

Date unknown

Adolph Hitler

I wish I could send some of my shock troops to Chicago and other big American cities to help with the elections. We look to Heinrich [sic] Ford as the leader of the growing Fascist movement in America. . . . We have just had his anti-Jewish articles translated and published. The book is being circulated in millions throughout Germany.[40]

Circa 1923

You can tell Herr Ford that I am a great admirer of his. I shall do my best to put his theories into practice in Germany.[41]

Circa 1923–29

I regard Henry Ford as my inspiration.[42]
Circa 1931

Al Jolson (1886–1950), Actor, Comedian, and Singer

Mr. Ford is a great man and he has done wonderful things.[43]
November 18, 1918, *New York Times*

Albert Kahn (1869–1942), Architect

He is a strange man. He seems to feel always that he is being guided by someone outside himself. With the simplicity of a farm hand discussing the season's crops, he makes vast moves.[44]
Circa 1920–29. Kahn, who was Jewish, refused to enter a Ford factory after 1920 because of Ford's anti-Semitism.

Fiorello La Guardia (1882–1947), Politician

The average Republican leader east of the Mississippi doesn't know anything more about Abraham Lincoln than Henry Ford knows about the Talmud.[45]
Circa 1922

Ring Lardner (1885–1933), Writer, Journalist, and Sports Commentator

Henry Ford once said he would rather be right than president, but I will go him one better and say I would rather have a Ford than be a Henry.[46]
Circa 1910–19

Charles Lindbergh (1902–1974), Aviator

Everytime [*sic*] I see Ford I am impressed by his eccentricity and his genius. How such genius succeeded is easy to understand, but how it carried such eccentricity along with it is more of a problem.[47]

Circa 1942

John Llewellyn Lewis (1880–1969), Union Leader

Henry Ford may believe that he is the biggest industrialist in America; he may believe that his will is superior to the will of his employe[e]s; he may believe that he is bigger than the United Automobile Workers; he may believe that he is bigger than the Congress of the United States when he refuses to abide by the Wagner Act enacted by the Congress; he may believe all these things, but if he does he is going to be a tired old man pretty soon.[48]

September 6, 1937, *Time*

Louis P. Lochner (1887–1975), Ford's Secretary, Journalist, and Author

Take any recent front-page picture or photograph of Henry Ford, and lay a sheet of paper on top . . . to cover one eye and one-half of his face. You will find that the left half is the face of the idealist, the dreamer, the humanitarian. Kindliness and good-will beam forth from the eye. There is something gentle about the expression. You are attracted at once to the man.

Then take the other half. It is the shrewd face of a sharp business man, alert, somewhat suspicious, somewhat cynical, full of cunning. The spiritual quality of the left eye gives place to a calculating materialism in the right.[49]

Circa 1925

Rev. Samuel S. Marquis, (1866–1948), Head of Ford's Sociological Department

The impression has somehow got around that Henry Ford is in the automobile business. It isn't true. Mr. Ford shoots about fifteen hundred cars out the back door of his factory every day just to get rid of them. They are but the by-products of his real business, which is the making of men.[50]

Circa 1916

The Ford car is Henry Ford done in steel, and other things. Not a thing of art and beauty, but of utility and strength.[51]

Circa 1923

Henry Ford appears to be drawn to the limelight as a moth to a candle. If he comes out slightly singed, as in the case of the Peace Ship and the *Tribune* trial, he nevertheless comes gaily and boldly back to flutter around a Semitic or other candle. One cannot but marvel at the continuance of the public's patience, interest and faith.[52]

Circa 1923

He has in him the makings of a great man, the parts lying about in more or less disorder. If only Henry Ford were properly assembled![53]

Circa 1923

Dr. Roy McClure, (1882–1951) Ford Family Physician

Henry Ford is a sick man, too. We must expect him to say and do unusual things.[54]

Circa 1943, advice to family members in the days leading up to Edsel's death

Alfred J. Murphy (1868–1931), Ford's Lawyer in the *Chicago Tribune* Lawsuit

The greatest humanitarian in the world.[55]

May 17, 1919, *New York Times*

New York Times

[H]e is an industrial Fascist—the Mussolini of Highland Park.[56]

January 8, 1928, *New York Times*

Diego Rivera (1886–1957), Mexican Artist

I should have attempted to write a book presenting Henry Ford as I saw him, a true poet and artist, and one of the greatest in the world.[57]

Circa 1932

Will Rogers (1879–1935), Humorist and Social Commentator

Yes, Mr. Ford is a fine feller. . . . I like him. He's a real he-man.[58]

Circa 1920–29

Henry Ford has always had more common sense than anybody.[59]

February 15, 1930, *New York Times*

He put wheels on our homes, a man's castle is his sedan. Life's greatest catastrophe is a puncture. . . . It will take a hundred years to tell whether he helped us or hurt us, but he certainly didn't leave us where he found us.[60]

Circa 1930–39

Franklin D. Roosevelt (1882–1945), American President

If Henry will quit being a damn fool . . . and call me on the telephone I would be glad to talk to him.[61]

Circa 1933–38, regarding an impasse over the National Recovery Act

Theodore Roosevelt (1858–1919), American President

Henry, like [P. T.] Barnum, has been a great advertiser.[62]
Circa 1910–19

Until he saw a chance for publicity free of charge, he thought a submarine was something to eat.[63]
Circa 1915, response to Ford's suggestion for a submarine design

Carl Sandburg (1878–1967), American Poet

One feels in talking with Ford that he is a man of power rather than of material riches.[64]
Circa December 1928

Aaron Sapiro (1884–1959), Lawyer Who Sued Ford for Libel

An industrialist, Henry Ford has made one of the greatest contributions ever made by any man. That is mass production. It amounts to first rate genius. But just as I am color blind, Henry Ford has blind spots in his intellect. In my opinion he is mentally unsound on certain questions of race and religion. He has a streak of bigotry on that side of his mind that is totally foreign to his industrial ability.[65]
March 28, 1927, *Time*

Charles M. Schwab (1862–1939), Steel Magnate

Henry Ford is the first man to promulgate the doctrine that for real prosperity in this country the working man should be prosperous. He not only promulgated it, but he put it into practice, and we followed.[66]
December 15, 1929, *New York Times*

Andre Siegfried (1875–1959),
French Historian and Academic

We can admire Ford, but we feel he is far removed from our ways, and at [the] bottom, he terrifies us.[67]

December 1930, *Review of Reviews*

Upton Sinclair (1878–1968), American Writer

He had never learned to deal with theories and when confronted with one, he would scuttle back to the facts like a rabbit to its hole.[68]

Circa 1937

Charles Sorensen (1881–1968),
Ford Motor Company Executive

It was useless to try to understand Henry Ford. One had to *sense* him.[69]

Date unknown

No, Henry Ford was not modest. . . . He pretended to be humble when with people who did not know him. But I knew this was an act.[70]

Date unknown

Joseph Stalin (1878–1953), Soviet Leader

[O]ne of America's greatest businessmen, Henry Ford. . . . I consider Mr. Ford one of the world's greatest industrialists. . . . [M]ay God preserve him.[71]

Circa September 1944

John Wanamaker (1838–1922), Merchant and Friend

Mr. Ford has three things—a mission, a generous heart, and a fat pocketbook; but he has no plan to stop the war.[72]

December 1, 1915, *New York Times*, reaction to Ford's Peace Ship

Woodrow Wilson (1856–1924), American President

You are the only man in Michigan who can be elected and help to bring about the peace you so much desire. I wish you therefore to overcome your personal feelings and interests and make the race [for senator].[73]

Circa June 1917

Stephen S. Wise (1874–1949), New York Rabbi

God pity and forgive Henry Ford . . . the most contemptible little liar that ever lived. . . . He is as guilty of pogroms as any murderer in Poland.[74]

November 13, 1920, *New York Times*

Frank Lloyd Wright

This is a man from whom the future had a right to expect something more than sentimentality.[75]

Circa late 1920–29, on Ford's abandonment of modern architecture under Albert Kahn and adoption of older styles

Notes

Preface and Acknowledgments

1. Sward, 116; see also Brinkley, 230; and Lacey, 160.
2. "Ford Asks Dealers to Pitch in and Help Roosevelt," *New York Times* (hereafter cited as *NYT*), Dec 8, 1933.
3. Charles Merz, "The Canonization of Henry Ford," *Dearborn Independent*, Nov 27, 1926, 524.
4. Kraft, 62.
5. "Autos: The Little Giant Goes," *Time*, Oct 8, 1945.
6. In addition to automobile parts, Ford had clothing made from his favorite bean.
7. Ford and Crowther, *My Life and Work*, 130.
8. "Ford Seeks a New Balance for Industry, *NYT*, May 29, 1932; see also "People, June 6, 1932," *Time*, Jun 6, 1932.
9. Comment made circa 1903. "Edison in His Laboratory," *Harper's Magazine*, Sept 1932, 406.
10. Lewis, 12.

Chapter 1. On Automobiles, Tractors, and Other Transportation Technology

1. Brinkley, 475.
2. Gelderman, 254.
3. Lewis, 203.
4. Ibid., 205.
5. Brinkley, 439.
6. Wik, 186.
7. Brinkley, 448.
8. Collier and Horowitz, 29.
9. Watts, 97; Collier and Horowitz, 49.

10. Bak, 38.
11. Ford and Crowther, *My Life and Work*, 72.
12. Ibid., 73.
13. Ibid., 272.
14. Wik, 59.
15. Collier and Horowitz, 417.
16. Beasley, 52.
17. Beasley and Stark, 216.
18. "Look into Future," *Boston Daily Globe*, Feb 16, 1913.
19. Lane, 94.
20. Collier and Horowitz, 49.
21. Henry Ford, "Why Henry Ford Wants to Be Senator," *World's Work*, Sept 1918, 524.
22. Collier and Horowitz, 64.
23. "Henry Ford, Dreamer and Worker," *Review of Reviews*, Nov 1921, 485.
24. Sward, 198, citing *Detroit News*, Nov 24, 1922.
25. "Ford Says Output Is 6,700 Cars a Day," *NYT*, May 30, 1923.
26. Stidger, 129.
27. Ford and Crowther, *My Life and Work*, 54.
28. Ibid., 57.
29. Ibid., 67.
30. "Henry Ford Says," *Motor*, Jan 1924, 70.
31. "Ford Backs His Ideas after Ten-Year Test," *NYT*, Aug 10, 1924.
32. "Henry Ford Predicts a Century of Prosperity," *NYT*, Sept 18, 1925.
33. Henry Ford, "Why I Favor Five Days' Work with Six Days' Pay," *World's Work*, Oct 1926, 614.
34. Ford and Crowther, *The Great To-Day and Greater Future*, 8.
35. Garrett, 69.
36. "Ford's Views on Europe's Needs," *NYT*, Jun 23, 1929.
37. Nevins and Hill, *Ford: Decline and Rebirth*, 16, citing *Detroit Times*, May 9, 1933.
38. Henry Ford, "Things I've Been Thinking About," *American Magazine*, Feb 1936, 21.
39. Gelderman 208, citing "The Ford Family," *Holiday*, Jun 1957, 72.
40. Newton, 99.
41. Collier and Horowitz, 197.
42. Ford and Crowther, *My Life and Work*, 36.

43. Jardim, citing *Detroit Free Press*, Jan 27, 1913. Similar quote: Brinkley, 342.
44. Nevins and Hill, *Ford: Expansion and Challenge*, 389.
45. Garrett, 66–67.
46. Ford and Crowther, *My Life and Work*, 70.
47. Newton, 99.
48. Collier and Horowitz, 123.
49. Ibid., 165.
50. "1,000 Fords a Day by Jan. 1, Says Ford," *NYT*, Dec 4, 1927.
51. "Henry Ford on His Plans and His Philosophy," *Literary Digest*, Jan 7, 1928, 44.
52. "Ford's Latest Invention," *NYT*, Jun 19, 1915.
53. "100,000 to Build Tractors," *NYT*, Mar 13, 1918.
54. "Henry Ford, Pacifist, Ready to Fight for Peace," *Literary Digest*, Apr 6, 1918, 83.
55. "How Power Will Set Men Free," *Popular Science*, Jul 1922, 26.
56. Stidger, 154.
57. "Ford's First Flight Is with Lindbergh," *NYT*, Aug 12, 1927.
58. "What of the Next 25 Years?" *Rotarian*, Jun 1936, 9.
59. "Ford's U-Flivver to Free the 7 Seas," *NYT*, Feb 10, 1917.
60. "Ford Thanks Ancients Had Planes and Radios," *NYT*, Dec 18, 1928; see also Trine, 78.

Chapter 2. On the Ford Motor Company, Business, and Management

1. Ford and Crowther, *My Life and Work*, 95.
2. Jaycox, 403; Wood, 70.
3. Rae, 24, citing the testimony in the 1916 suit between the Dodge Brothers and Ford.
4. Ford and Crowther, *My Life and Work*, 100.
5. Ibid., 112.
6. Marquis, 153–54.
7. Lacey, 274.
8. William Stidger, "Put the Bible Back in School," *Good Housekeeping*, Apr 1924, 241.
9. William S. Dutton, "Wages Will Go Up and Prices Come Down Says Henry Ford," *American Magazine*, Jul 1928, 15–16.
10. Nevins and Hill, *Ford: Expansion and Challenge*, 439.

11. "Ford Reveals Plan for Great Output," *NYT*, Feb 28, 1932. Similar quote: "Business: Ford Risks All," *Time*, Mar 7, 1932, 55.
12. "Ford Sits Up in Bed, Talks of a New Car," *NYT*, Dec 2, 1932.
13. "Ford Asserts Pay Must Be Increased," *NYT*, Jun 16, 1933.
14. Bennett, 271.
15. Richards, 160.
16. Bennett, 167.
17. Collier and Horowitz, 83.
18. "Henry Ford Discusses the Wage," *State Service: The New York State Magazine*, Feb 1919.
19. Kraft, 54.
20. "Henry Ford Wants Cowless Milk and Crowdless Cities," *Literary Digest*, Feb 26, 1921, 42; see also Ford and Crowther, *My Life and Work*, 11.
21. Ford, *Ford Ideals*, 16.
22. Ibid., 30.
23. Ibid., 52.
24. Ibid., 53.
25. Ford and Crowther, *My Life and Work*, 44.
26. Ibid., 45.
27. Ibid., 49.
28. Ibid., 92.
29. Ibid.
30. Ibid., 130.
31. Ibid., 160.
32. Ibid., 160.
33. Ibid., 233.
34. Ibid., 263.
35. Marquis, 156.
36. Ibid., 157.
37. "Henry Ford Tells Why He Supports Calvin Coolidge," *Boston Daily Globe*, Oct 31, 1924.
38. Untitled article, *System*, Jan 1926, 106.
39. Ford and Crowther, *The Great To-Day and Greater Future*, 13.
40. Ibid., 33. Similar quote: ibid., 20.
41. Ibid., 26.
42. "Comings & Goings: May 21, 1928," *Time*, May 21, 1928.
43. Ford and Faurote, *My Philosophy of Industry*, 21.

44. "Foundations of Prosperity," *North American Review*, Aug 1929, 135.
45. Ford, *Moving Forward*, 7.
46. Newton, 101.
47. Henry Ford, "Things I've Been Thinking About," *American Magazine*, Feb 1936, 17.
48. Wallace, 10.
49. Newton, 114.
50. "Mr. Ford's Page," *Dearborn Independent*, Nov 14, 1925, 9.
51. Samuel Crowther, "Our Job," *Saturday Evening Post*, Oct 31, 1936, 6.
52. "Ford, 78, Predicts Post-War Gains," *NYT*, Jul 29, 1941.
53. Lane, 161.
54. "Henry Ford's Pet Plans," *Boston Daily Globe*, Dec 4, 1921.
55. Ford, *Ford Ideals*, 20.
56. Ibid., 34.
57. Ibid., 76.
58. Ibid., 79.
59. Ford and Crowther, *My Life and Work*, 130.
60. Ford, Ibid., 97.
61. Ford, Ibid., 263.
62. "How Henry Ford Manages," *Literary Digest*, Jan 16, 1926, 22.
63. Ibid.
64. Ibid.
65. "Henry Ford Writes a Utopia in Terms of Machinery," *NYT*, Jul 11, 1926.
66. Ibid.
67. "Morgan, Wilson & Ford," *Review of Reviews*, Jul 1936, 34.
68. Ford and Crowther, *My Life and Work*, 52.
69. Brinkley, 234, citing *Detroit News*, Nov 10, 1911. Later included in Ford and Crowther, *My Life and Work*, 16.
70. Ford and Crowther, *My Life and Work*, 91.
71. Ibid., 92.
72. "Henry Ford, Dreamer and Worker," *Review of Reviews*, Nov 1921, 493.
73. Ford and Crowther, *My Life and Work*, 28.
74. Ibid., 86.
75. Ford Motor Company, *The Ford Industries,* 119.
76. Ford and Crowther, *My Life and Work*, 41.
77. Ibid., 185.
78. Garrett, 104.

79. Henry Ford, "Why Henry Ford Wants to Be Senator," *World's Work*, Sept 1918, 523.

80. Jardim, 93, citing *Detroit Times*, Nov 14, 1916; Rae, 27–28, citing *Detroit News*, Nov 4, 1916.

81. Ibid.

82. Ford and Crowther, *My Life and Work*, 20.

83. "Henry Ford Tells Us We Should Work," *NYT*, May 16, 1926.

84. "No Age Limit of Work, Says Ford at 65 . . . ," *NYT*, Jul 31, 1928.

85. "Henry Ford Favors One Big Power Trust," *NYT*, Jul 7, 1929.

86. Ford and Crowther, *My Life and Work*, 45.

87. Nye, 75, citing *System*, May 1924, 611.

88. Ford and Crowther, *The Great To-Day and Greater Future*, 22.

89. "Faith in Older Men Stressed by Ford," *NYT*, May 20, 1930.

90. "Sales Methods That Net $1,000,000 a Week," *System*, Mar 1917, 512.

91. "Henry Ford, Dreamer and Worker," *Review of Reviews*, Nov 1921, 494.

92. Ibid. Later in Ford and Crowther, *My Life and Work*, 58.

93. "Business: Cut It Out . . . ," *Time*, Aug 9, 1926, 27.

94. "Henry Ford Tells Us We Should Work," *NYT*, May 16, 1926.

95. Trine, 96.

96. Garrett, 67.

97. Lane, 50.

98. Ford and Crowther, *My Life and Work*, 275.

99. Ford and Crowther, *The Great To-Day and Greater Future*, 27.

100. "The Duel of the Motor Giants," *Literary Digest*, Aug 20, 1927.

101. William S. Dutton, "Wages Will Go Up and Prices Come Down Says Henry Ford," *American Magazine*, Jul 1928, 111.

102. Ibid.

103. "Henry Ford Looks at the World," *NYT*, Oct 26, 1930.

104. Baldwin, 269.

105. "What of the Next 25 Years?" *Rotarian*, Jun 1936, 47.

Chapter 3. On Money and Economics

1. For more on Ford's prejudice against Jews, please see the section in chapter 15 titled "On Jews."

2. Lacey, 165.

3. Lane, vi.

4. Ibid., 132.

5. From the first issue of the *Dearborn Independent*, Jan 11, 1919; Nevins and Hill, *Ford: Expansion and Challenge*, 127.

6. William S. Dutton, "Wages Will Go Up and Prices Come Down Says Henry Ford," *American Magazine*, Jul 1928, 15. Similar quote: Ford and Crowther, *My Life and Work*, 157; regarding money as a tool for self improvement, see also: "Henry Ford Talks to Young Men," *American Magazine*, Aug 1929, 158.

7. William S. Dutton, "Wages Will Go Up and Prices Come Down Says Henry Ford," *American Magazine*, Jul 1928, 15.

8. "Henry Ford Talks to Young Men," *American Magazine*, Aug 1929, 160.

9. "Business & Finance: Motormaker Looks at Life," *Time*, Feb 24, 1930.

10. "Hoarded Funds Lost, Asserts Henry Ford," *NYT*, Nov 8, 1931.

11. "Henry Ford Plans for a New Adventure," *NYT*, Mar 26, 1933.

12. James C. Derieux, "Faith in the Future," *Good Housekeeping*, Jul 1933.

13. Nevins and Hill, *Ford: Decline and Rebirth*, 14. Similar quote: "Henry Ford Plans for a New Adventure," *NYT*, Mar 26, 1933.

14. "My Faith in the Future," *Rotarian*, Aug 1942, 11.

15. "Ford's Sayings Reveal Life's Philosophy," *Toledo (Ohio) Blade*, Apr 8, 1947.

16. "Henry Ford Has Changed Views," *Boston Daily Globe*, Jan 3, 1916.

17. "Ford Says He Kept His Son from War," *NYT*, Jul 24, 1919.

18. William L. Stidger, "Henry Ford's Ideal: People before Profits," *Outlook,* May 9, 1923, 845. Similar quote: Ford, *Ford Ideals*, 71.

19. "Who IS Henry Ford?" *Time*, May 19, 1923, 7.

20. "People, June 4, 1934," *Time*, Jun 4, 1934.

21. Richards, 1, citing *New York Herald*.

22. "Ford's Advice to Boys," *NYT*, Jan 25, 1919.

23. "Henry Ford, Dreamer and Worker," *Review of Reviews*, Nov 1921, 482.

24. Ibid.

25. Ford and Crowther, *My Life and Work*, 223.

26. Newton, 101.

27. "National Affairs: Like a Dream," *Time*, May 9, 1938, 10.

28. Olson, 179.

29. "Ford Challenges 'Fertilizer Trust,'" *NYT*, Jan 15, 1922.

30. Garrett, 68.

31. "Mr. Ford's Page," *Dearborn Independent*, Nov 14, 1925.

32. "Ford Scans the Economic Scene," *NYT*, May 24, 1931.

33. Ibid.
34. "Hoarded Funds Lost, Asserts Henry Ford," *NYT*, Nov 8, 1931. Similar quote: "The Promise of the Future Makes the Present Seem Drab," *NYT*, Sept 13, 1931.
35. Samuel Crowther, "The Only Real Security: An Interview with Henry Ford," *Saturday Evening Post*, Feb 1, 1936, 58.
36. "Ford, Denying Hate, Lays War to Jews," *NYT*, Oct 29, 1922. Similar quote: Miller, 55.
37. Ford and Crowther, *My Life and Work*, 176.
38. Ibid., 177.
39. "Times Good, Not Bad, Ford Says . . . ," *NYT*, Feb 1, 1933.
40. "Banks: Close to Bottom," *Time*, Mar 6, 1933, 19.
41. "Ford, at 80, Expounds His Faith," *NYT*, Jul 25, 1943.
42. Benson, 191. (Note: Gelderman, 362, interview from the same date says "Jew speculators," instead of "Wall Street.")
43. "Henry Ford Sums up Political Outlook," *NYT*, Oct 19, 1924.
44. Ford and Crowther, *My Life and Work*, 7.
45. "Ford Decries Debts of Credit System," *NYT*, Jun 20, 1926.
46. "Business & Finance: Motormaker Looks at Life," *Time*, Feb 24, 1930.
47. "Ford Says High Pay Will End Slump," *NYT*, May 29, 1930.
48. Samuel Crowther, "There Is No Santa Claus," *Saturday Evening Post*, May 16, 1931, 25.
49. Ibid., 97.
50. Ford Decries Debts of Credit System," *NYT*, Jun 20, 1926.
51. "'I Believe in Reincarnation'—Henry Ford," *Milwaukee Sentinel*, Aug 4, 1928.
52. Henry Ford Explains Why He Gives Away $10,000,000," *NYT*, Jan 11, 1914.
53. Lewis, 11.
54. Charles W. Wood, "I Asked Mr. Ford If He Would Run for President. He Says:—," *Collier's*, Aug 26, 1922, 6.
55. Marquis, 36.
56. Henry Ford, "America Has Just Started," *World's Work*, June 1928, 208.
57. Ford and Crowther, *My Life and Work*, 19.
58. Wik, 88.
59. "Ford Says High Pay Will End Slump," *NYT*, May 29, 1930.
60. Sward, 224.
61. "International: Ford Is Mohammed," *Time*, Oct 13, 1930.

62. "Prosperity Is Up to People Ford Asserts," *Fort Myers (Fla.) Press*, Mar 15, 1931.
63. "Ford Calls Slump 'Wholesome Thing,'" *NYT*, Oct 21, 1931.
64. "Ford at 69 Predicts a Happy America," *NYT*, Jul 31, 1932.
65. "Ford Predicts Upturn," *NYT*, Aug 28, 1932.
66. Wik, 188.
67. "Times Good, Not Bad, Ford Says . . . ," *NYT*, Feb 1, 1933.
68. Nevins and Hill, *Ford: Decline and Rebirth*, 16, citing *Detroit Times*, Apr 16, 1933.
69. "Ford Asserts Pay Must Be Increased," *NYT*, Jun 16, 1933.
70. James C. Derieux, "Faith in the Future," *Good Housekeeping*, Jul 1933.
71. "Ford: Urging 'Common Sense,' He Waves Aside Depression," *Newsweek*, Nov 10, 1934, 34.

Chapter 4. On Employees and Ford's Social Policies

1. Gartman, 88.
2. Lewis and Goldstein, 18.
3. Jacques, 27.
4. Hooker, 71.
5. Brinkley, 390–91.
6. "Henry Ford's Experiment in Good-Will," *Everybody's Magazine*, Apr 1914, 469. Similar quote: "Gives $10,000,000 to 26,000 Employe[e]s," *NYT*, Jan 4, 1914.
7. "Henry Ford's Experiment in Good-Will," *Everybody's Magazine*, Apr 1914, 469.
8. Watts, 185.
9. Rae, 20, citing the testimony in the 1916 suit between the Dodge Brothers and Ford.
10. Lane, 150–51.
11. Ibid., 165.
12. "Henry Ford on Victory by Tool-Power," *Literary Digest*, May 4, 1918, 27.
13. Ford, *Ford Ideals*, 79.
14. Ford and Crowther, *My Life and Work*, 80.
15. Ibid., 99.
16. Ibid., 99.
17. Ibid., 114.
18. Stidger, 90.

19. "Ford, Edison, Firestone Jolly Coolidge Callers," *Boston Daily Globe*, Aug 20, 1924.

20. Ford and Crowther, *The Great To-Day and Greater Future*, 11.

21. Ford and Faurote, *My Philosophy of Industry*, 16–17.

22. "Henry Ford," *New Republic*, Nov 14, 1923, 303.

23. "Ten Millions [*sic*] Now in Ford Peace Fund," *NYT*, Sept 9, 1915.

24. Nevins and Hill, *Ford: Expansion and Challenge*, 36.

25. Ford and Crowther, *My Life and Work*, 107.

26. Stidger, 64.

27. Ibid.

28. Henry Ford, "Give American Youth a Chance," *World's Work*, Dec 1926, 209.

29. "Henry Ford Explains Why He Gives Away $10,000,000," *NYT*, Jan 11, 1914.

30. Henry Ford, "Highways to Mastery as Observed by a Master Builder," *Current Opinion*, Oct 1922, 467. Also in: Ford, *Ford Ideals*, 50.

31. Henry Ford, *Ford Ideals, Being a Selection from "Mr. Ford's Page," in the Dearborn Independent*, 50.

32. Ford and Crowther, *My Life and Work*, 120.

33. Ibid., 147.

34. "Foreign News: Ford Abroad," *NYT*, Apr 7, 1930.

35. "Ford Scans the Economic Scene," *NYT*, May 24, 1931.

36. Ibid.

37. Nevins and Hill, *Ford: Decline and Rebirth*, 65.

38. Samuel Crowther, "The Only Real Security: An Interview with Henry Ford," *Saturday Evening Post*, Feb 1, 1936, 58.

39. "Henry Ford Explains Why He Gives Away $10,000,000," *NYT*, Jan 11, 1914.

40. Watts, 182, quoting *Detroit Free Press*, Jan 6, 1914.

41. Ibid., 185.

42. Henry Ford, "Why Henry Ford Wants to Be Senator," *World's Work*, Sept 1918, 526.

43. Newton, 102.

44. "Forty-Hour Week Settled Policy of Henry Ford Plant," *Akron (Ohio) Weekly Pioneer Press*, May 5, 1922.

45. "Ford Backs His Ideas after Ten-Year Test," *NYT*, Aug 10, 1924.

46. "Mr. Ford's Page," *Dearborn Independent*, Nov 13, 1926. Similar quote: *Iron Trade Review*, Nov 1926, 1296.

47. "Business: Harvester Holidays," *Time*, Jan 14, 1929.
48. "Squalid Homes Banned by Ford," *NYT*, Apr 19, 1914.
49. "Henry Ford's Experiment in Good-Will," *Everybody's Magazine*, Apr 1914, 469.
50. Ibid.
51. "Ford Praises President," *NYT*, Sept 3, 1916.
52. "Ford Plans Great Wilson Propaganda," *NYT*, Oct 7, 1916.
53. Lane, 75–76. Similar quote: "The Great American Enigma," *Harper's Magazine*, Oct 1930, 514.
54. Ford, *Ford Ideals*, 57.
55. "Ford Defends Life in Industrial Age," *NYT*, Jul 30, 1930.
56. "Henry Ford Predicts Auto Plans Will Go on Ten-Month Year," *NYT*, Aug 10, 1930. Similar quote: Samuel Crowther, "There Is No Santa Claus," *Saturday Evening Post*, May 16, 1931.
57. Samuel Crowther, "There Is No Santa Claus," *Saturday Evening Post*, May 16, 1931.
58. "Ford Scans the Economic Scene," *NYT*, May 24, 1931. Similar quote: Samuel Crowther, "There Is No Santa Claus," *Saturday Evening Post*, May 16, 1931.
59. "National Affairs: Mayors, Misery & Money," *Time*, Jun 13, 1932, 13.
60. "Henry Ford Explains Why He Gives Away $10,000,000," *NYT*, Jan 11, 1914.
61. "Henry Ford Gives Strange Interview," *Boston Daily Globe*, May 24, 1916.
62. "Ford Praises President," *NYT*, Sept 3, 1916.
63. Lane, 127–28.
64. "Muzzle Financiers, Henry Ford Advises," *NYT*, Aug 10, 1922.
65. "Henry Ford, Dreamer and Worker," *Review of Reviews*, Nov 1921, 493.
66. "Ford Calls I.C.C. Wall Street Pawn," *NYT*, Sept 14, 1922.
67. Nevins and Hill, *Ford: Expansion and Challenge*, 353.
68. "Ford Sees Peril in Secret Bigotry," *NYT*, Oct 31, 1925. Similar comment: "Ford Says His Men May 'Join Anything,'" *NYT*, Apr 14, 1937.
69. "'Happiness on the Road,' Declares Henry Ford," *Boston Daily Globe*, May 11, 1926.
70. "A German Visits Henry Ford," *Living Age*, October 1930, 158, citing *Berliner Tageblatt*.
71. Ibid.
72. Newton, 101.

73. "Ford Is Considering Making Car Bodies," *NYT*, Jan 29, 1933.

74. "Labor: Body Strike," *Time*, Feb 6, 1933.

75. "Ford Says His Men May 'Join Anything,'" *NYT*, Apr 14, 1937. Similar comments in Nevins and Hill, *Ford: Decline and Rebirth*, 49.

76. "National Affairs: Motor Peace," *Time*, Apr 19, 1937, 16.

77. "Labor: Strikes-of-the-Week," *Time*, May 24, 1937, 12.

78. Burlingame, 140.

79. Nevins and Hill, *Ford: Decline and Rebirth*, 136–37, citing *Detroit News*, Apr 29, 1937; see also Ford Motor Company, *Ford Gives Viewpoint on Labor, Cautions Workers on Organization*, 3.

80. Brinkley, 426.

81. Sorensen, 260.

82. "Ford Sees Unions 'Losing Ground,'" *NYT*, Mar 9, 1941.

83. "Labor: Model T Tycoon," *Time*, Mar 17, 1941, 19.

84. Collier and Horowitz, 169; Sorensen, 267.

85. Lewis, 432.

Chapter 5. On Work and Leisure

1. "Commercialism Made This War," NYT, Apr 11, 1915.

2. Ibid.

3. Lane, 161.

4. "Henry Ford Discusses the Wage," *State Service: The New York State Magazine*, Feb 1919, 34. Similar statement: Ford and Crowther, *My Life and Work*, 120

5. "Henry Ford Discusses the Wage," *State Service: The New York State Magazine*, Feb 1919, 34.

6. Ibid.

7. Ford and Crowther, *My Life and Work*, 45.

8. Ibid., 120.

9. Marquis, 153.

10. Ibid., 38–39.

11. Benson, 262.

12. Ibid., 296.

13. "Ford Backs His Ideas after Ten-Year Test," *NYT*, Aug 10, 1924.

14. "'Happiness on the Road,' Declares Henry Ford," *Boston Daily Globe*, May 11, 1926.

15. Ford and Crowther, *The Great To-Day and Greater Future*, 18. Similar

quotes: "Ford Tells the Aim of His 5-Day Week," *NYT*, Oct 11, 1926; Nevins and Hill, *Ford: The Times, the Man, the Company*, 579.

16. Jerome Davis, "Henry Ford, Educator," *Atlantic Monthly*, Jun 1927, 803.

17. "Think Big, Henry Ford Advises Young Men," *NYT*, Oct 1, 1927.

18. "Ford Praises Jews in Talk with Editor," *NYT*, Nov 21, 1927.

19. Trine, 156.

20. "'I Believe in Reincarnation'—Henry Ford," *Milwaukee Sentinel*, Aug 4, 1928.

21. "Ford Urges for Farms New Mass Production," *NYT*, Mar 7, 1930.

22. "The Great American Enigma," *Harper's Magazine*, Oct 1930, 514.

23. Ford, *Moving Forward*, 90.

24. "Prosperity Is up to People Ford Asserts," *Fort Myers (Fla.) Press*, Mar 15, 1931.

25. Samuel Crowther, "There Is No Santa Claus," *Saturday Evening Post*, May 16, 1931, 96. Similar quote: "Labor: Model T Tycoon," *Time*, Mar 17, 1941, 19.

26. "Ford Sees Recovery in Work and Thought," *NYT*, Jul 26, 1931.

27. "Ford Seeks a New Balance for Industry, *NYT*, May 29, 1932.

28. Samuel Crowther, "The Only Real Security: An Interview with Henry Ford," *Saturday Evening Post*, Feb 1, 1936, 58.

29. Henry Ford, "Things I've Been Thinking About," *American Magazine*, Feb 1936, 17.

30. Sept 21, 1938, entry in Howard Simpson's diary, in Nevins and Hill, *Ford: Decline and Rebirth*, 124.

31. "Ford Faces Forward," *Rotarian*, Sept 1944, 14.

32. Benson, 308.

33. "Henry Ford Predicts a Century of Prosperity," *NYT*, Sept 18, 1925.

34. "'Happiness on the Road,' Declares Henry Ford," *Boston Daily Globe*, May 11, 1926.

35. "Ford, Back, Paints Big Future in Air," *NYT*, May 9, 1928.

36. William S. Dutton, "Wages Will Go Up and Prices Come Down Says Henry Ford," *American Magazine*, Jul 1928, 112.

37. Ford and Crowther, *My Life and Work*, 103.

38. Ibid., 105.

39. Ibid., 53.

40. "Henry Ford Talks to Young Men," *American Magazine*, Aug 1929, 158.

41. Lane, 24.

42. Ford and Crowther, *My Life and Work*, 13.
43. Ibid., 278.
44. "Henry Ford Tells Us We Should Work," *NYT*, May 16, 1926.
45. Ford and Crowther, *Today and Tomorrow*, 220.
46. Trine, 26.
47. "Labor: Model T Tycoon," *Time*, Mar 17, 1941, 115.
48. Richards, 4.
49. Henry Ford, "Thinking Out Loud," *American Magazine*, Oct 1934, 154.
50. Harding, 41. Similar quote: Trine, 128.
51. Dahlinger, 63.
52. Quoting a dancing manual produced by Ford. "Henry Ford Shakes a Wicked Hoof," *Literary Digest*, Aug 15, 1925, 38.
53. "Ford Revives the Old Dances," *NYT*, Aug 16, 1925.
54. Ibid.
55. Ibid.
56. Nevins and Hill, *Ford: Expansion and Challenge*, 491–92.

Chapter 6. On Machines and Technology

1. "The Great American Enigma," *Harper's Magazine*, Oct 1930, 524.
2. Ford, *Ford Ideals*, 39–40.
3. Ford and Crowther, *My Life and Work*, 1.
4. Ibid., 2.
5. Ibid., 24.
6. "'Happiness on the Road,' Declares Henry Ford," *Boston Daily Globe*, May 11, 1926.
7. "Ford Tells the Aim of His 5-Day Week," *NYT*, Oct 11, 1926.
8. Nye, 123.
9. Ford and Faurote, *My Philosophy of Industry*, 18; Trine, 78.
10. "Ford Raps Tariff, Extols Free Trade," *NYT*, Apr 11, 1928. Similar quote: "The Unsung Heroes," *Popular Mechanics*, Aug 1928, 202.
11. "Ford Says High Pay Will End Slump," *NYT*, May 29, 1930.
12. "Ford Says Machine Can Never Oust Man," *NYT*, Mar 17, 1931.
13. "Ford Scans the Economic Scene," *NYT*, May 24, 1931.
14. Ibid.
15. Ibid.
16. "Times Good, Not Bad, Ford Says . . . ," *NYT*, Feb 1, 1933.
17. Ibid.

18. "What of the Next 25 Years?" *Rotarian*, Jun 1936, 8. Similar quote: "Ford, at 80, Expounds His Faith," *NYT*, Jul 25, 1943.

19. Wik, 101.

20. Ford and Crowther, *My Life and Work*, 148–49.

21. Collier and Horowitz, 55.

22. "Ford Would Oust Bankers and Parasitic R.R. Stockholders," *Current Opinion*, Jan 1922, 112. Similar quote: "Henry Ford, Dreamer and Worker," *Review of Reviews*, Nov 1921, 493.

23. Trine, 80.

24. "What of the Next 25 Years?" *Rotarian*, Jun 1936, 6.

25. "My Faith in the Future," *Rotarian*, Aug 1942, 12.

Chapter 7. On Politics and Government

1. Pipp, 18–19.

2. "Henry Ford Has Changed Views," *Boston Daily Globe*, Jan 3, 1916.

3. "Ford Plans Great Wilson Propaganda," *NYT*, Oct 7, 1916. Similar quote: circa 1916, Nevins and Hill, *Ford: Expansion and Challenge*, 117.

4. Brinkley, 229.

5. Merz, 225. Similar quote: "I, Too, Was a Murderer,' Says Ford," *New York Tribune*, Jul 17, 1919.

6. "I, Too, Was a Murderer,' Says Ford," *New York Tribune*, July 17, 1919.

7. Ford, *Ford Ideals*, 29.

8. Ford and Crowther, *My Life and Work*, 7.

9. Ibid., 8.

10. Ibid.

11. "Henry Ford Sums Up Political Outlook," *NYT*, Oct 19, 1924.

12. Ford and Crowther, *The Great Today and Greater Future*, 338

13. "Ford Hails Hoover as Leader of Age," *NYT*, Sep 8, 1928.

14. "Prosperity Is up to People Ford Asserts," *Fort Myers (Fla.) Press*, Mar 15, 1931.

15. Samuel Crowther, "There Is No Santa Claus," *Saturday Evening Post*, May 16, 1931, 96.

16. "Ford Seeks a New Balance for Industry," *NYT*, May 29, 1932.

17. James C. Derieux, "Faith in the Future," Jul 1933.

18. Samuel Crowther, "The Only Real Security: An Interview with Henry Ford," *Saturday Evening Post*, Feb 1, 1936, 6.

19. Ibid.

20. "Republicans: Going Places," *Time*, Oct 26, 1936, 16.
21. "Model T Meeting," *Newsweek*, May 9, 1938, 11.
22. "Henry Ford Urges Election of Wilson," *NYT*, Sept 28, 1916. Similar quote: "Henry Ford Comes Out for Wilson," *Boston Daily Globe*, Sept 15, 1916.
23. Merz, 222.
24. "Ford Looks for Coolidge to Win," *Boston Daily Globe*, Feb 12, 1924.
25. Henry Ford, "Concerning 'Preparedness,'" *Toledo (Ohio) Blade*, Mar 2, 1916.
26. "The 'Appalling Simplicity' of Henry Ford," *Current Opinion*, Nov 1916, 313. Similar statement: Henry A. Wise Wood, "A Wild Mental Journey with Ford," *NYT*, May 17, 1916.
27. "Henry Ford at Bay: The Extraordinary Trial at Mr. Clemens," *Forum*, Aug 1919, 140.
28. Henry Ford, "Why Henry Ford Wants to Be Senator," *World's Work*, Sept 1918, 253.
29. "Henry Ford Back, Denies Deserting," NYT, Jan 3, 1916.
30. A Unique Forgetfulness," *NYT*, Jun 23, 1918.
31. "National Affairs: Famous Last Words," *Time*, Nov 9, 1936, 14.
32. "Ford Says High Tax on Rich Hurts Poor," *NYT*, Feb 25, 1924.
33. Ibid.
34. Ibid.
35. "Henry Ford Urges Election of Wilson," *NYT*, Sept 28, 1916. Similar quote: "Great Britain: High Tea," *Time*, Apr 23, 1928.
36. "Tariff 'an Excuse for Laziness,' Ford's Parting Word to Britain," *NYT*, Oct 18, 1930.
37. "Henry Ford Explains Why He Gives Away $10,000,000," NYT, Jan 11, 1914.
38. Ford and Crowther, *My Life and Work*, 5.
39. Samuel Crowther, "Foundations of Prosperity," interview with Henry Ford, *North American Review*, Aug 1929, 130.
40. Richards, 246.
41. Lacey 384.
42. Henry Ford, "Why Henry Ford Wants to Be Senator," *World's Work*, Sept 1918, 522.
43. Ibid. Similar quote: "Urged by Wilson, Ford Accepts," *NYT*, Jun 14, 1918.
44. Lewis, 98. Similar quotes: Henry Ford, "Why Henry Ford Wants to Be

Senator," *World's Work*, Sept 1918, 522; "Ford Disavows Party Pledges," *NYT*, Sept 26, 1918, 522.

45. Leonard, 138.
46. Ibid., 137.
47. "Ford Says $176,000 Beat Him at Polls," *NYT*, Nov 16, 1918.
48. Benson, 307.
49. Nevins and Hill, *Ford: Expansion and Challenge*, 303.
50. Ibid.
51. "No Presidency for Ford," *NYT*, Feb 7, 1914.
52. *NYT*, Mar 2, 1916.
53. Bryan, *Clara: Mrs. Henry Ford*, 185.
54. Henry Ford, "Why Henry Ford Wants to Be Senator," *World's Work*, Sept 1918, 522.
55. "The Jewish Bloc in Mr. Ford's Presidential Path," *Literary Digest*, Aug 25, 1923.
56. "Imaginary Interviews," *Time*, May 28, 1923; see also Stidger, 85.
57. "Ford Might Run If a Crisis Came," *NYT*, Aug 1, 1923.
58. "Henry Ford," *New Republic*, Nov 14, 1923.

Chapter 8. On War and Peace

1. Nevins and Hill, *Ford: Expansion and Challenge*, citing *New York Herald*, Jan 23, 1915.
2. "Commercialism Made This War," *NYT*, Apr 11, 1915.
3. Ibid.
4. Gelderman, 92; see also "Commercialism Made This War," *NYT*, Apr 11, 1915.
5. "Commercialism Made This War," *NYT*, Apr 11, 1915.
6. Ibid.
7. Ibid.
8. Baldwin, 49, citing *Detroit News*, Jun 18, 1915.
9. "Ford to Start Peace Campaign," *NYT*, Aug 23, 1915.
10. Ibid.
11. Nye, 15, citing *Detroit Times*, Aug 22, 1915.
12. "Ford Opposes War Loan," *NYT*, Sept 19, 1915.
13. Sward, 86, citing *Detroit News*, Nov 15, 1915.
14. Nov 26, 1915. Nevins and Hill, *Ford: Expansion and Challenge*, 36. Similar quotes: "Ford Gets His Ship; Seeks 'Live Wires,'" *NYT*, Nov 28, 1915. For more, see Kraft, 67–70.

15. "Ford Hires Liner in Peace Crusade," *NYT*, Nov 25, 1915. Similar quotes: "Ford Condemns War, Blames Capitalism," *NYT*, Nov 15, 1915; "Ford Says His Purpose Is a Strike in the Trenches," *NYT*, Nov 30, 1915.

16. "Henry Ford in Search of Peace," *Literary Digest*, citing *New York Sun*, Dec 11, 1915, 1335.

17. Richards, 37. Similar quote: "Ford Willing to Give Fortune to End War," *NYT*, Nov 24, 1915.

18. "Henry Ford Back, Denies Deserting," *NYT*, Jan 3, 1916.

19. Ibid.

20. Henry Ford, "Concerning 'Preparedness,'" *Toledo (Ohio) Blade*, Mar 2, 1916.

21. Gelderman, 177. Similar quote later in the war: *NYT*, July 17, 1919.

22. From a telegram sent to the New York Republican Club, Jan 17, 1917; Leonard, 127.

23. "Industries Put at Nation's Call," *NYT*, Feb 6, 1917. Similar quotes: circa Apr 1917. Nevins and Hill, *Ford: Expansion and Challenge*, 57; "Ford Ready to Show He's Senate Timber," *NYT*, Jun 23, 1918; "Henry Ford, Master of Efficiency," *Independent*, Feb 19, 1917, 293; "Henry Ford Takes $5,000,000 of Bonds," *NYT*, Oct 17, 1917.

24. Lane, 177.

25. Ibid., 176.

26. Henry Ford, "Why Henry Ford Wants to Be Senator," *World's Work*, Sept 1918, 523.

27. Ibid., 522.

28. "Ford Says He Kept His Son from War," *NYT*, Jul 24, 1919.

29. "Ford Hopes to Use Muscle Shoals as Step to End Wars," NYT, Dec 4, 1921. Similar quote: Ford and Faurote, *My Philosophy of Industry*, 66.

30. Ford and Crowther, *My Life and Work*, 242.

31. Stidger, 181.

32. "Millions of Planes Soon, Ford Predicts," *NYT*, Jul 21, 1924.

33. "Henry Ford Tells Us We Should Work," *NYT*, May 16, 1926.

34. "Henry Ford Assails the Death Penalty," *NYT*, Feb 5, 1927.

35. "Ford Raps Tariff, Extols Free Trade," *NYT*, Apr 11, 1928.

36. "Business & Finance: Motormaker Looks at Life," *Time*, Feb 24, 1930.

37. Richards, 219.

38. Samuel Crowther, "The Only Real Security," *Saturday Evening Post*, Feb 1, 1936, 6.

39. "National Affairs: Shadows," *Time*, Sept 11, 1939, 16.

40. "National Affairs: Big Michigander," *Time*, Oct 2, 1939, 16.
41. "Life on the Newsfronts of the World," *Life*, Dec 16, 1940, 24.
42. Collier and Horowitz, 180.
43. "Battle of Detroit," *Time*, Feb 9, 1942.
44. "My Faith in the Future," *Rotarian*, Aug 1942, 10.
45. Ibid., 12.
46. Ibid.
47. "People: Casualties," *Time,* 44, citing *Atlanta Constitution*, Mar 27, 1944.
48. "Ford Faces Forward," *Rotarian*, Sept 1944, 16.
49. "100,000 to Build Tractors," *NYT*, Mar 13, 1918.
50. Ford Gratified at Progress in Beautification," *Fort Myers (Fla.) Press*, Feb 20, 1929.
51. "Ford's Sayings Reveal Life's Philosophy," *Toledo (Ohio) Blade*, Apr 8, 1947.
52. Nevins and Hill, *Ford: Expansion and Challenge*, 39.
53. Leonard, 91.
54. For more on press reactions and public opinion, see Gelderman, 107; and Alvarado and Alvarado, 50.
55. Nevins and Hill, *Ford: Expansion and Challenge*, 41.
56. Baldwin, 25.
57. "Ford Abandons Peace Party to Sail for Home," *Toledo (Ohio) Blade*, Dec 30, 1915.
58. "Ford Is Preparing New Peace Project," *NYT*, Feb 7, 1916.
59. Henry Ford, "Why Henry Ford Wants to Be Senator," *World's Work*, Sept 1918, 522.
60. Stidger, 25.
61. "Commercialism Made This War," *NYT*, Apr 11, 1915. Similar quote: "Ford Says Soldiers Are Murderers, *NYT*, Jul 16, 1919.
62. "Commercialism Made This War," *NYT*, Apr 11, 1915. Similar quotes: "Quizzing of Ford Ends after 7 Days," *NYT*, Jul 23, 1919; "Ford Says He Kept His Son from War," *NYT*, Jul 24, 1919.
63. Gelderman, 92, citing *Detroit Times*, Apr 19, 1916.
64. Leonard, 126.
65. "Quizzing of Ford Ends after 7 Days," *NYT*, Jul 23, 1919.
66. "Ford Faces Forward," *Rotarian*, Sept 1944, 16.
67. Ford, *Ford Ideals*, 60.
68. "Ford Urges Army Keep Country 'Dry,'" *NYT*, Jun 10, 1923.

69. "Ford to Start Peace Campaign," *NYT*, Aug 23, 1915.

70. Henry Ford, "Why Henry Ford Wants to Be Senator," *World's Work*, Sept 1918, 523; "Industries Put at Nation's Call," *NYT*, Feb 6, 1917. Similar quotes: "Should Build Ships on Standard Model," *Boston Daily Globe*, Nov 18, 1917.

71. Gelderman, 169.

Chapter 9. On Law, the Legal System, Crime and Punishment

1. Lacey, 267.

2. "Ford Seldom Reads below Headlines," *NYT*, Jul 19, 1919.

3. Ford and Crowther, *My Life and Work*, 7.

4. Henry Ford, "Thinking Out Loud," *American Magazine*, Oct 1934, 18.

5. Bennett, 122.

6. "Ford, at 80, Expounds His Faith," *NYT*, Jul 25, 1943.

7. "The Jewish Bloc in Mr. Ford's Presidential Path," *Literary Digest*, Aug 25, 1923, 51.

8. Ibid.

9. "Henry Ford, Dreamer and Worker," *Review of Reviews*, Nov 1921, 493. Similar quote: Greenleaf, 114.

10. "Ten Millions [*sic*] Now in Ford Peace Fund," *NYT*, Sept 9, 1915. Similar quote about idleness: "'Happiness Is on the Road' Declares Henry Ford," *Boston Daily Globe,* May 11, 1926.

11. "Henry Ford Tells Us We Should Work," *NYT*, May 16, 1926.

12. Henry Ford, "Give American Youth a Chance," *World's Work*, Dec 1926, 207.

13. "To Turn 'Yearners' into Workers," *Literary Digest*, Mar 1, 1930, 9.

14. Elizabeth Breuer, "Henry Ford and the Believer," *Ladies' Home Journal,* Sept 1923, 8.

15. Ibid.

16. Ibid.

17. Watts, 339.

18. "Henry Ford Assails the Death Penalty," *NYT*, Feb 5, 1927.

19. Ibid.

20. Wik, 221, citing *St. Louis Daily Globe Democrat*, Feb 3, 1927.

21. "Ford Against Execution," *NYT*, Aug 10, 1927.

22. "Henry Ford's Pet Plans," *Boston Daily Globe*, Dec 4, 1921.

23. "Ford's 'Freeze-Out' of Rail Partners Blocked by I.C.C.," *NYT*, Mar 11, 1922.

Chapter 10. On Education and the Arts

1. Galbraith, 144.
2. "A Talk with Henry Ford," *Harper's Weekly*, May 29, 1915, 518.
3. Lane, 169.
4. Ibid., 170.
5. Ibid., 170–71.
6. Simonds, *Henry Ford and Greenfield Village*, 57–58.
7. "Henry Ford, Dreamer and Worker," *Review of Reviews*, Nov 1921, 484.
8. Allan F. Wright, "Opportunity Beacons to Young Bank Men," *Bankers Magazine*, Mar 1922, 467.
9. Ford and Crowther, *My Life and Work*, 249.
10. "Ford Revives the Old Dances," *NYT*, Aug 16, 1925.
11. "High Jinks on Edison's Eightieth Birthday," *Literary Digest*, Mar 5, 1927, 38.
12. Jerome Davis, "Henry Ford, Educator," *Atlantic Monthly*, Jun 1927, 803. Similar quote: James C. Derieux, "The Making of an American Citizen," *Good Housekeeping*, Oct 1934, 121.
13. Jerome Davis, "Henry Ford, Educator," *Atlantic Monthly*, Jun 1927, 803.
14. "No Successful Boy Saves Money . . . ," *NYT*, Dec 14, 1928. Similar quote: Nevins and Hill, *Ford: Expansion and Challenge*, 610.
15. Trine, 36.
16. "Business & Finance: Motormaker Looks at Life," *Time*, Feb 24, 1930, 9.
17. "Ford Defends Life in Industrial Age," *NYT*, Jul 30, 1930.
18. "The Great American Enigma," *Harper's Magazine*, Oct 1930, 523.
19. "Ford Says Machine Can Never Oust Man," *NYT*, Mar 17, 1931.
20. James C. Derieux, "The Making of an American Citizen," *Good Housekeeping*, Oct 1934, 117.
21. Ibid.
22. "Mr. Ford Shows His Museum," *NYT*, Jan 12, 1936.
23. "Henry Ford, Schoolmaster," *Reader's Digest*, Sept 1938, 100.
24. "Ford's Advice to Boys," *NYT*, Jan 25, 1919.
25. "'I am Ignorant of Most Things,' Ford Declares," *New York Tribune*, July 19, 1919.
26. "Quizzing of Ford Ends after 7 Days," *NYT*, Jul 23, 1919.

27. "Mr. Ford's First Reader," *NYT*, Oct 23, 1921.

28. Marquis, 56.

29. Benson, 330.

30. Trine, 35.

31. "Ford Defends Life in Industrial Age," *NYT*, Jul 30, 1930.

32. "The Great American Enigma," *Harper's Magazine*, Oct 1930, 523.

33. "What of the Next 25 Years?" *Rotarian*, Jun 1936, 6.

34. "Michigan: Detroit Dynasty," *Time*, Apr 21, 1947, 28.

35. Wik, 9.

36. Lacey, 260.

37. Behrman, 166.

38. "'Happiness on the Road,' Declares Henry Ford," *Boston Daily Globe*, May 11, 1926.

39. Circa 1933. Rivera, 120.

40. Henry Ford, "Thinking Out Loud," *American Magazine*, Oct 1934, 19.

41. "Start the Day with a Song," *Etude*, Apr 1936.

Chapter 11. On History, the Past, and Museums

1. Interview by Charles Wheeler, *Chicago Tribune*, May 25, 1916.

2. Nevins and Hill, *Ford: Expansion and Challenge*, 138.

3. "The 'Appalling Simplicity' of Henry Ford," *Current Opinion*, Nov 1916, 313.

4. Ibid.

5. Lane, 33.

6. "Henry Ford's 1940 World," *Hearst's International*, Jan 1922, 72. Similar quote: "Ford Defends Life in Industrial Age," *NYT*, Jul 30, 1930.

7. Ford, *Ford Ideals*, 10.

8. "Ford Looks for Coolidge to Win," *Boston Daily Globe,* Feb 12, 1924.

9. "Ford to Show How the Colonists Lived," *NYT*, Feb 12, 1924.

10. Circa Feb 1924. Wallace, 10.

11. Circa Feb 1924. Sward, 104; "I, Too, Was a Murderer,' says Ford," *New York Tribune*, July 17, 1919.

12. "Ford Revives the Old Dances," *NYT*, Aug 16, 1925.

13. Ibid.

14. Trine, 31.

15. Ibid., 88.

16. Newton, 102.

17. James C. Derieux, "Faith in the Future," *Good Housekeeping*, Jul 1933.

18. Ibid.
19. James C. Derieux, "The Making of an American Citizen," *Good Housekeeping*, Oct 1934, 117.
20. "Mr. Ford Shows His Museum," *NYT*, Jan 12, 1936.
21. "Ford, at 80, Expounds His Faith," *NYT*, Jul 25, 1943. Similar quote: "Looking under the Human Hood," *Rotarian*, Jan 1947, 56.
22. Brinkley, 511.
23. "Ford's Sayings Reveal Life's Philosophy," *Toledo (Ohio) Blade*, Apr 8, 1947.
24. Bryan, *Clara: Mrs. Henry Ford,* 203. Similar quote: Lacey, 239.
25. Trine, 31.
26. "Ford Builds a Unique Museum," *NYT*, Apr 5, 1931. Similar quote: Ford, *Today and Tomorrow*, 225.
27. Collier and Horowitz, 108. Similar quote: Trine, 30.
28. "Mr. Ford Shows His Museum," *NYT*, Jan 12, 1936. Similar quote: Henry Ford Museum and Greenfield Village, Education Dept, 116.
29. Wik, 207.
30. Ibid., 208.

Chapter 12. On the Press

1. See "On Jews" in chapter 15.
2. "Ford Abandons Peace Party to Sail for Home," *Toledo (Ohio) Blade*, Dec 30, 1915.
3. "Henry Ford Rues Peace Trip," *NYT*, Jan 4, 1916.
4. "Henry Ford Gives Strange Interview," *Boston Daily Globe*, May 24, 1916.
5. Stidger, 132.
6. Benson, 335.
7. "Ford Sees Coolidge on Muscle Shoals," *NYT*, Dec 4, 1925.
8. "Henry Ford on His Plans and His Philosophy," *Literary Digest*, Jan 7, 1928, 48.
9. Ibid., 48.
10. "Ford Back, Declines to be Interviewed," *NYT*, Oct 23, 1930.
11. Bennett, 84.
12. Ibid., 154.
13. "Henry Ford Retires as Motor Plant's Head," *NYT*, Nov 23, 1918.
14. Baldwin, 78.
15. "Ford Explains Attacks," *NYT*, Dec 5, 1921. Similar quote: Upton

Sinclair, "Henry Ford Tells Just How Happy His Great Fortune Made Him," *Reconstruction*, May 1919, 129.

16. "Races: Apology to Jews," *Time*, Jul 18, 1927, 12.

Chapter 13. On Humanity

1. Nevins and Hill, *Ford: Expansion and Challenge*, 40.
2. Lane, vi.
3. Ibid., 105.
4. Ibid., 156. Similar quote: ibid., 165.
5. Lane, 128.
6. Henry Ford, "Why Henry Ford Wants to Be Senator," *World's Work*, Sept 1918, 523.
7. Bonville, citing *Dearborn Independent*, May 24, 1919, 13.
8. Garrett, 79.
9. Ford, *Ford Ideals*, 21. Similar quote: Stidger, 207.
10. Ford and Crowther, *The Great To-Day and Greater Future*, 3.
11. Trine, 35.
12. "Ford Says High Pay Will End Slump," *NYT*, May 29, 1930.
13. "The Promise of the Future Makes the Present Seem Drab," *NYT*, Sept 13, 1931.
14. "Hoarded Funds Lost, Asserts Henry Ford," *NYT*, Nov 8, 1931.
15. Ford, *Ford Ideals*, 42.
16. Ibid., 78.
17. Ford and Crowther, *My Life and Work*, 44.
18. Ibid., 95.
19. Ibid., 220.
20. "'Happiness on the Road,' Declares Henry Ford," *Boston Daily Globe*, May 11, 1926. Also variation: "Henry Ford Tells Us We Should Work," *NYT*, May 16, 1926.
21. Nevins and Hill, *Ford: Expansion and Challenge*, 619.
22. "My Faith in the Future," *Rotarian*, Aug 1942, 12.
23. Ford, *Ford Ideals*, 307.
24. Elizabeth Breuer, "Henry Ford and the Believer," *Ladies' Home Journal*, Sept 1923, 8.
25. Ibid.
26. Ibid., 122.
27. Ibid.
28. Ibid.

29. Ford and Crowther, *My Life and Work*, 111.
30. James C. Derieux, "Faith in the Future," *Good Housekeeping*, Jul 1933.
31. Bennett, 65.
32. Sorensen, 271.
33. "Ford Faces Forward," *Rotarian*, Sept 1944, 16.
34. "Looking under the Human Hood," *Rotarian*, Jan 1947, 9.
35. Lane, 45.
36. Ford, *Ford Ideals*, 74.
37. "Business & Finance: Motormaker Looks at Life," *Time*, Feb 24, 1930. Similar quote: "Henry Ford's Experiment in Good-Will," *Everybody's Magazine*, Apr 1914, 468.
38. Elizabeth Breuer, "Henry Ford and the Believer," *Ladies' Home Journal*, Sept 1923, 8.
39. "Henry Ford's Pet Plans," *Boston Daily Globe*, Dec 4, 1921.
40. Wik, 205.
41. "Henry Ford at 62D Milestone," *Boston Daily Globe*, Jul 30, 1925.
42. "'Happiness on the Road,' Declares Henry Ford," *Boston Daily Globe*, May 11, 1926.
43. "No Age Limit of Work, Says Ford at 65 . . . ," *NYT*, Jul 31, 1928.
44. William S. Dutton, "Wages Will Go Up and Prices Come Down Says Henry Ford," *American Magazine*, Jul 1928, 15.
45. Trine, 71.
46. Ibid., 150.
47. Ibid.
48. Samuel Crowther, "When is a Man Old? An Interview with Henry Ford," *Ladies' Home Journal*, Jul 1929, 25. Also in: Ford, *Moving Forward*, 7. Similar quote: Henry Ford, "Thinking Out Loud," *American Magazine*, Oct 1934, 19.
49. James C. Derieux, "Faith in the Future," *Good Housekeeping*, Jul 1933.
50. Ibid.
51. "Henry Ford at 73 Goes to Lake Lodge . . . ," *NYT*, Jul 30, 1936.
52. Stidger, 50.
53. Henry Ford, "Give American Youth a Chance," *World's Work*, Dec 1926, 207.
54. Ibid.
55. Ford and Faurote, *My Philosophy of Industry*, 12–13.
56. "Faith in Older Men Stressed by Ford," *NYT*, May 30, 1930.
57. Ibid.

58. "Henry Ford Seeks to Make Thinkers," *NYT*, Aug 9, 1931.

59. "Ford for Youth in Office," *NYT*, Mar 12, 1941.

60. "Looking Under the Human Hood," *Rotarian*, Jan 1947, 9.

61. Ibid., 10.

62. Nye, 60.

Chapter 14. On Religion, Reincarnation, and Charity

1. Richards, 149.

2. Baldwin, 38.

3. "Henry Ford in Search of Peace," *Literary Digest*, Dec 11, 1915, 1335.

4. Lane, 8.

5. "Ford, Denying Hate, Lays War to Jews," *NYT*, Oct 29, 1922.

6. William Stidger, "Put the Bible Back in School," *Good Housekeeping*, Apr 1924, 83.

7. Ibid., 240.

8. Ibid.

9. "Ford Revives the Old Dances," *NYT*, Aug 16, 1925.

10. "Ford Sees Peril in Secret Bigotry," *NYT*, Oct 31, 1925.

11. Lacey, 234. Similar quote: Trine, 22.

12. Lacey, 235.

13. Ford was probably referring to Orlando Smith's (1842–1908) *Eternalism, A Theory of Infinite Justice*, published in 1902.

14. "Religion: Reincarnationist," *Time*, Sept 3, 1928, 42.

15. Ibid.

16. Trine, 141.

17. Ibid., 143. Similar quote: "Ford Sees Peril in Secret Bigotry," *NYT*, Oct 31, 1925.

18. Trine, 144.

19. Ibid., 144–45.

20. Ibid., 170.

21. "Ford Says He Reads Bible Every Day," *NYT*, Jul 25, 1929, citing *Christian Herald*, Jul 1929.

22. Richards, 149.

23. Bennett, 220.

24. Ibid., 210.

25. "Ford, at 80, Expounds His Faith," *NYT*, Jul 25, 1943.

26. Nye, 94.

27. Benson, 108. Similar quote: ibid., 110.

28. Lacey, 234.

29. "Henry Ford Master Mind Sends Message to Earth," *San Francisco Examiner*, Aug 26, 1928; Nye, 103; Lacey, 59.

30. Trine, 178.

31. Bak, 42.

32. "Ford Seeks a New Balance for Industry," *NYT*, May 29, 1932. Also "People, June 6, 1932," *Time*, Jun 6, 1932, 22.

33. Bennett, 83.

34. Collier and Horowitz, 132.

35. Nye, 59.

36. Bennett, 287.

37. Ibid., 30.

38. Watts, 184.

39. Circa 1917. Nevins and Hill, *Ford: Expansion and Challenge*, 36.

40. Lane, 144.

41. "Henry Ford 'Off Charity for Life,'" *Boston Daily Globe*, Nov 19, 1918.

42. Ibid.

43. Wik, 228.

44. "Ford Says His Road Pays the Wage Rise," *NYT*, Jul 29, 1921.

45. Ford, *Ford Ideals*, 62. Similar quote: Wik, 228.

46. Ibid., 62.

47. Ibid., 63.

48. Ibid., 45.

49. "Henry Ford," *New Republic*, Nov 14, 1923, 5.

50. Ford and Crowther, *My Life and Work*, 206.

51. Marquis, 104

52. Stidger, 36.

53. "High Jinks on Edison's Eightieth Birthday," *Literary Digest*, Mar 5, 1927, 34.

54. "Ford's Sayings Reveal Life's Philosophy," *Toledo (Ohio) Blade*, Apr 8, 1947.

55. Bennett, 30.

56. Kraft, 44, citing one of Ford's jot books.

57. "A Talk with Henry Ford," *Harper's Weekly*, May 29, 1915, 520.

58. Wik, 175, citing *Collier's*, Aug 26, 1923, 6.

59. Benson, 272.
60. Ford and Crowther, *My Life and Work*, 3.

Chapter 15. On Nations, Nationalities, Ethnic and Religious Groups, and the United States

1. Lane, 176.
2. Circa 1917. Nevins and Hill, *Ford: Expansion and Challenge*, 80.
3. Ford, *Ford Ideals*, 23.
4. In response to the "Mexican-Catholic question." "Ford Criticizes Wets," *NYT*, Jun 23, 1929.
5. "Looking under the Human Hood," *Rotarian*, Jan 1947, 10.
6. "Squalid Homes Banned by Ford," *NYT*, Apr 19, 1914.
7. Baldwin, 80, quoting *Dearborn Independent*, Feb 22, 1919.
8. Dahlinger, 159.
9. Bennett, 83.
10. Ibid., 87.
11. "Ford Praises Jews in Talk with Editor," *NYT*, Nov 21, 1927.
12. "Barthhold Cancels Consent," *NYT*, Dec 1, 1915.
13. "Ford Says High Tax on Rich Hurts Poor," *NYT*, Feb 25, 1924.
14. "'Happiness on the Road,' Declares Henry Ford," *Boston Daily Globe*, May 11, 1926. Similar quote: "Ford Abroad," *World's Work*, December 1931, 48.
15. "Ford Sailing Today; Raises Berlin Wages," *NYT*, Oct 17, 1930.
16. "Henry Ford," *New Republic*, Nov 14, 1923, 7.
17. "Ford, Edison, Firestone Jolly Coolidge Callers," *Boston Daily Globe*, Aug 20, 1924.
18. Wallace, 27, citing *Detroit Free Press*, circa July 1922.
19. "Ford, Denying Hate, Lays War to Jews," October 29, 1922.
20. "Henry Ford," *New Republic*, Nov 14, 1923, 303.
21. Pipp, 27
22. Wallace, 15.
23. Graves, *The Truth about "The Protocols: a Literary Forgery*," exposes "The Protocols" as a plagiarized version of an 1864 Maurice Joly publication by a paragraph-by-paragraph comparison of the texts.
24. Wallace, 15.
25. Bryan, *Beyond the Model T*, 104.
26. Wallace, 2.

27. Gelderman, 223.

28. Harry Bennett claimed that Ford never read the apology (Bennett, 56). Conot's *American Odyssey*, 239, claims Henry Ford never signed the agreement; Harry Bennett did.

29. "Commercialism Made This War," *NYT*, Apr 11, 1915.

30. "Ford Plans to Save Mexico by Work," *NYT*, Jul 26, 1922.

31. Ford and Crowther, *My Life and Work*, 4.

32. "Ford Praises Jews in Talk with Editor," *NYT*, Nov 21, 1927.

33. "History Is Bunk, Says Henry Ford," *NYT*, Oct 29, 1921.

34. Ford, *Ford Ideals*, 66.

35. Stidger, 106. Similar quote: Trine, 38.

36. Ford and Faurote, *My Philosophy of Industry*, 3.

37. "Ford Hails Hoover as Leader of Age," *NYT*, Sep 8, 1928.

38. "Ford Scans the Economic Scene," *NYT*, May 24, 1931.

39. "Ford, on Air, Urges Election of Hoover," *NYT*, Oct 20, 1932.

40. Samuel Crowther, "The Only Real Security: An Interview with Henry Ford," *Saturday Evening Post*, Feb 1, 1936, 6.

41. Ibid., 58.

42. Samuel Crowther, "Our Job," *Saturday Evening Post*, Oct 31, 1936, 5.

43. Newton, 114.

44. "Henry Ford Opens Doors of Wayside Inn to G.A.R.," *Boston Daily Globe*, Aug 11, 1924.

45. "Ford Sits Up in Bed, Talks of a New Car," *NYT*, Dec 2, 1932.

46. Nevin and Hill, *Ford: Expansion and Challenge*, 610.

47. Marquis, 38.

48. Nevins and Hill, *Ford: Expansion and Challenge*, 479 citing *Detroit Saturday Night*, Jun 24, 1916.

49. "Henry Ford Contributes to Fund for Rookeries in Alligator Bay," *Fort Myers (Fla.) Press*, Mar 5, 1914.

50. "National Affairs: Dirty Work at Dearborn," *Time*, Mar 24, 1930.

51. Ford and Crowther, *My Life and Work*, 192.

52. Stidger, 155.

53. "Ford Backs His Ideas after Ten-Year Test," *NYT*, Aug 10, 1924.

54. "Business & Finance: Motormaker Looks at Life," *Time*, Feb 24, 1930. Similar quote: James Derieux, "Faith in the Future," *Good Housekeeping*, Jul 1933.

55. James C. Derieux, "Faith in the Future," *Good Housekeeping*, Jul 1933.

Chapter 16. On Health

1. Lane, 156.
2. Stidger, 125. Similar quotes: Lane, 79; "People, December 5, 1932," *Time*, Dec 5, 1932, 56.
3. Trine, 114.
4. Ibid., 117.
5. Ibid., 126.
6. Stidger, 100.
7. "'Happiness on the Road,' Declares Henry Ford," *Boston Daily Globe*, May 11, 1926.
8. Bryan, *Clara: Mrs. Henry Ford*, 238.
9. Frank Parker Stockbridge, "Henry Ford, Amateur," *World's Work*, Sept 1918, 510. Similar quote: Marquis, 108.
10. Greenleaf, 54.
11. Benson, 309. Similar quote: Ford and Crowther, *My Life and Work*, 216.
12. Trine, 75.
13. "Detroit the Dynamic," *Collier's*, Jul 4, 1914, 26.
14. Benson, 265.
15. "Farmers Should Work Only 25 Days a Year, Says Henry Ford," *Boston Daily Globe*, Sept 14, 1924.
16. "Henry Ford Says People Can Live to Be 125, But Must Quit Tea, Coffee, Tobacco, Liquor," *NYT*, Aug 15, 1924.
17. "Henry Ford Says 'There is Always Room for More,'" *Popular Science*, Feb 1925, 154.
18. "Ford Says Strike Was 'Put Over,'" *NYT*, May 11, 1926.
19. "Henry Ford Tells Us We Should Work," *NYT*, May 16, 1926.
20. Ford, *My Philosophy of Industry*, 10–11.
21. Trine, 111.
22. Ibid., 112.
23. Ibid., 114.
24. Ibid., 128.
25. "Ford Wants Diet Taught by the Clergy; Holds Right Food Will Cut Illness and Crime," *NYT*, May 10, 1929, quoting *Red Book Magazine*, Jun 1929.
26. "Ford Defends Life in Industrial Age," *NYT*, Jul 31, 1930.
27. Richards, 294.

28. Bennett, 284.

29. "Henry Ford Nears 81st Birthday Looking to Future," *Evening Independent,* Jul 28, 1944.

30. Nye, 65.

31. Ford and Crowther, *My Life and Work*, 54.

32. Ibid.

33. Wik, 152.

34. Nye, 64.

35. "The 'Appalling Simplicity' of Henry Ford," *Current Opinion*, Nov 1916, 312.

36. Ibid.

37. Lane, 28.

38. "Mr. Ford's Philosophy," *NYT*, Jun 1, 1919.

39. Stidger, 198, 200; "Ford Urges Army Keep Country 'Dry,'" *NYT,* Jun 10, 1923.

40. "Ford Favors a 'Dry' Coolidge," *Boston Daily Globe*, Oct 26, 1923.

41. Richards, 157. Similar quote: Ford and Faurote, *My Philosophy of Industry*, 14–15.

42. "Ford Raps Tariff, Extols Free Trade," *NYT*, Apr 11, 1928.

43. "Ford Says Nation Is Too Fast to Be Wet," *NYT*, Aug 18, 1928. Similar quotes: "National Affairs: Dirty Work at Dearborn," *Time*, Mar 24, 1930; "Ford and Booze Won't Mix," *Literary Digest*, Sept 7, 1929, 7; "People: September 2, 1929," *Time*, Sept 2, 1929.

44. "Ford Says Dry Law Guards Prosperity," *NYT*, Nov 3, 1928.

45. Ibid.

46. Ford and Faurote, *My Philosophy of Industry*, 15. Similar quotes: Trine, 135; "Ford Criticizes Wets," *NYT*, Jun 23, 1929.

47. "Ford Wants Diet Taught by the Clergy; Holds Right Food Will Cut Illness and Crime," *NYT*, May 10, 1929, quoting from *Red Book Magazine*, Jun 1929.

48. "Ford Says He Reads Bible Every Day," *NYT*, Jul 25, 1929, citing *Christian Herald*, Jul 1929.

49. Ibid.

50. "Edison and Ford Head Opposition to Dry Repeal," *Fort Myers (Fla.) Press*, Mar 6, 1930.

51. "National Affairs: Dirty Work at Dearborn," *Time*, Mar 24, 1930.

52. Nevins and Hill, *Ford: Expansion and Challenge*, 489. Similar quote: "International: Ford Is Mohammed," *Time*, Oct 13, 1930.

53. "The 'Appalling Simplicity' of Henry Ford," *Current Opinion*, Nov 1916, 313.

54. Ford, *The Little White Slaver*, 4.

55. Ibid.

Chapter 17. On Nature, Science, Energy, and Fuel

1. Lewis, 282–83.

2. "Henry Ford Prophesies the Doom of the Horse," *Los Angeles Herald*, May 3, 1908.

3. "Henry Ford Prophesies the Doom of the Horse," *Los Angeles Herald*, May 3, 1908. Similar quotes: Nevins and Hill, *Ford: The Times, the Man, the Company*, 183, citing Detroit *News-Tribune*, Feb 4, 1900. See also Bak, 36.

4. "Henry Ford Goes to See the Start," *NYT*, Jan 12, 1914.

5. "Ford's Platform Out: 'No Place Like Home,'" *Literary Digest*, Jul 14, 1923, 38.

6. "Farmers Should Work Only 25 Days a Year, Says Henry Ford," *Boston Daily Globe*, Sept 14, 1924. Similar quote: "Henry Ford Wants Cowless Milk and Crowdless Cities," *Literary Digest*, Feb 26, 1921, 42.

7. "Farmers Should Work Only 25 Days a Year, Says Henry Ford," *Boston Daily Globe*, Sept 14, 1924. Similar quote: Wik, 147, citing the 1925 *Farm and Fireside*.

8. "Farmers Should Work Only 25 Days a Year, Says Henry Ford," *Boston Daily Globe*, Sept 14, 1924. Similar quote: "Henry Ford Wants Cowless Milk and Crowdless Cities," *Literary Digest*, Feb 26, 1921, 42.

9. Dahlinger, 171. Similar quote: Nye, 80, citing *Detroit News*, Jul 16, 1936.

10. Dahlinger, 172.

11. Watts, 19. Similar quotes: Bak, 31, 36.

12. Watts, 184.

13. "Ford Sees Victory with Small Tanks, *NYT*, Mar 25, 1918.

14. Frank Parker Stockbridge, "Henry Ford, Amateur," *World's Work*, Sept 1918, 515.

15. "Henry Ford, Dreamer and Worker," *Review of Reviews*, Nov 1921, 483.

16. Ford and Crowther, *My Life and Work*, 99.

17. Ibid., 22.

18. Edgar A. Guest, "Henry Ford Talks about His Mother," *American Magazine*, Jul 1923, 120.

19. Ford and Crowther, *My Life and Work*, 26. Similar quotes: "Once They

Walked in the Fields," *Life*, Sept 1, 1952, 62; Ford and Faurote, *My Philosophy of Industry*, 9.

20. Stidger, 153.

21. Ibid., 155. Similar quote: "City's Doom Near; Henry Ford's View," *NYT*, Aug 28, 1924.

22. "Farmers Should Work Only 25 Days a Year, Says Henry Ford," *Boston Daily Globe*, Sept 14, 1924.

23. Ibid. Similar quotes: Ford and Faurote, *My Philosophy of Industry*, 8; Trine, 89; "Ford Says Machine Can Never Oust Man," *NYT*, Mar 17, 1931.

24. Merz, 221.

25. "Ford Predicts Fuel from Vegetation," *NYT*, Sept 20, 1925, citing *Christian Science Monitor*.

26. Ford Decries Debts of Credit System," *NYT*, Jun 20, 1926.

27. Samuel Crowther, "There Is No Santa Claus," *Saturday Evening Post*, May 16, 1931, 98. Similar quotes: Nye, 81; "Times Good, Not Bad, Ford Says . . . ," *NYT*, Feb 1, 1933. Similar quotes: "Labor: Threat Averted," *Time*, Feb 13, 1933, 13; Henry Ford, "Thinking Out Loud," *American Magazine*, Oct 1934, 154; "What of the Next 25 Years?" *Rotarian*, Jun 1936, 6.

28. Samuel Crowther, "There Is No Santa Claus," *Saturday Evening Post*, May 16, 1931, 98.

29. Wik, 192, citing *Christian Science Monitor*, Apr 1933. Similar quote: "Times Good, Not Bad, Ford Says . . . ," *NYT*, Feb 1, 1933.

30. Nye, 82.

31. Henry Ford, "Why Henry Ford Wants to Be Senator," *World's Work*, Sept 1918, 526.

32. "Ford Orders Family Men at Michigan to Grow Own Vegetables . . . ," *NYT*, Aug 24, 1931.

33. Ibid.

34. Gelderman, 290; Lewis, 233. Similar quotes: "My Faith in the Future," *Rotarian*, Aug 1942, 12; "Ford Uses Company in Back-to-Land Farm Plan, . . . ," *NYT*, May 8, 1932.

35. Nevins and Hill, *Ford: Expansion and Challenge*, 610

36. "Mr. Ford Tells for Plans for Stronger Cars," *Popular Science*, Mar 1941, 128.

37. "Ford Will Sell Lumber at Cost," *NYT*, Oct 26, 1923. Similar quote: Stidger, 160.

38. Grandin, 62.
39. Henry Ford, "America Has Just Started," *World's Work*, June 1928, 208.
40. "How Power Will Set Men Free," *Popular Science*, Jul 1922, 24.
41. Henry Ford, "Why Henry Ford Wants to Be Senator," *World's Work*, Sept 1918, 525. Similar quote: Brinkley, 219, citing *Detroit News*, Jul 12, 1916.
42. "How Power Will Set Men Free," *Popular Science*, Jul 1922, 26.
43. Henry Ford, "America Has Just Started," *World's Work*, June 1928, 209.
44. "Henry Ford, Dreamer and Worker," *Review of Reviews*, Nov 1921, 488. Similar quote: "Ford Predicts Fuel from Vegetation," *NYT*, Sept 20, 1925.
45. Henry Ford, "Why Henry Ford Wants to Be Senator," *World's Work*, Sept 1918, 526. Similar quote: "History Is Bunk, Says Henry Ford," *NYT*, Oct 29, 1921. Similar quotes: "Henry Ford's Great Ambition," *Illustrated World*, May 1922, 348; Nye, 84, 348; "Henry Ford's Great Ambition," *Illustrated World*, May 1922, 349.
46. Segal, 21. Similar quote: Stidger, 138.

Chapter 18. On Family

1. Watts, 16.
2. Bak, 8.
3. Edgar Guest, "Henry Ford Talks About His Mother," *American Magazine*, Jul 1923, 14. Similar quote: "Ford's Platform Out: 'No Place Like Home,'" *Literary Digest*, Jul 14, 1923, 37.
4. "'I Believe in Reincarnation,'—Henry Ford," *Milwaukee Sentinel*, Aug 4, 1928; "Labor: Model T Tycoon," *Time*, Mar 17, 1941.
5. Ford and Crowther, *My Life and Work*, 24. Similar quote: Allan Benson, "The Intimate Life of Henry Ford," *Hearst's International*, Dec 1922, 22.
6. Collier and Horowitz, 48.
7. Ibid., 27.
8. Dahlinger, 69.
9. Allan L. Benson, "The Intimate Life of Henry Ford," *Hearst's International*, Dec 1922, 23. Another source says he never took advice from Clara: Elizabeth Breuer, "Henry Ford and the Believer," *Ladies' Home Journal*, Sept 1923, 122.
10. Elizabeth Breuer, "Henry Ford and the Believer," *Ladies' Home Journal*,

Sept 1923, 8. Similar quotes: "Looking under the Human Hood," *Rotarian*, Jan 1947, 9; Ford, *My Life and Work*, 30.

11. Newton, 118.

12. Sorensen, 268–69.

13. Lacey, 191; slightly different wording in "Henry Ford on Heaven," *Saturday Evening Post*, Aug 16, 1947, 128.

14. Clancy and Davies, 121.

15. "Topics of the Times," *NYT*, Jan 9, 1914.

16. "Henry Ford Explains Why He Gives Away $10,000,000," *NYT*, Jan 11, 1914. Similar quotes: "Henry Ford Retires as Motor Plan's Head," *NYT*, Nov 23, 1918; "Henry Ford's Pet Plans," *Boston Daily Globe*, Dec 4, 1921.

17. Circa 1926. Lacey, 291.

18. "Henry Ford Talks about Edsel and Edsel Talks about his Father," *World's Work*, Aug 1928, 392.

19. Sorensen, 318.

20. Gelderman, 218.

21. Bennett, 292.

22. Gelderman, 215.

23. Richards, 232.

Chapter 19. On Himself

1. Trine, 52.

2. Lane, 16.

3. Ibid., 175.

4. Nevins and Hill, *Ford: The Times, the Man, the Company*, 586; see also Marquis, 169.

5. "The 'Appalling Simplicity' of Henry Ford," *Current Opinion*, Nov 1916, 312.

6. Ibid., 313.

7. "'I, Too, Was a Murderer,' Says Ford," *New York Tribune*, July 17, 1919.

8. Baldwin, 77.

9. Ford and Crowther, *My Life and Work*, 103.

10. "Ford, Denying Hate, Lays War to Jews," *NYT*, Oct 29, 1922.

11. Ibid.

12. William L. Stidger, "Henry Ford's Ideal: People Before Profits," *Outlook*, May 9, 1923, 845.

13. "Ford Urges Army Keep Country 'Dry,'" *NYT*, Jun 10, 1923.

14. "Henry Ford Seen through a Reducing Glass," *Current Opinion*, Sept 1923, 326.
15. Stidger, 57.
16. "'Choose' Means No to Ford," *NYT*, Dec 5, 1927.
17. Trine, 52.
18. "Ford Finds Wealth Unsettling to Men," *NYT*, Aug 28, 1929. Similar quote: "Ford Defends Life in Industrial Age," *NYT*, Jul 30, 1930.
19. Richards, 146. Similar quote: ibid., 148.
20. "Mr. Ford Shows His Museum," *NYT*, Jan 12, 1936.
21. Ibid.
22. Richards, 208.
23. Sorensen, 30.
24. Collier and Horowitz, 22.
25. Nye, 96.
26. Bryan, *Henry's Lieutenants*, 11.
27. Newton, 101.
28. Collier and Horowitz, 70.
29. "Edison Batteries for New Ford Cars," *NYT*, Jan 11, 1914.
30. Gelderman, 60.
31. "The Great American Enigma," *Harper's Magazine*, Oct 1930, 523.
32. Dahlinger, 159

Chapter 20. On Miscellaneous Topics

1. Ford, *My Life and Work*, 13.
2. Ford and Crowther, *The Great To-Day and Greater Future*, 20.
3. "Ford Sees Peril in Secret Bigotry," *NYT*, Oct 31, 1925. Similar quotes: Richards, 152; "Ford Sees Peril in Secret Bigotry," *NYT*, Oct 31, 1925.
4. "Ford Thinks Ancients Had Planes and Radios," *NYT*, Dec 18, 1928, citing *McClure's Magazine*, Jan 1928, 115; Trine, 76.
5. "Speaking of Pictures," *Life*, Jun 5, 1939, 9.
6. "Henry Ford, Dreamer and Worker," *Review of Reviews*, Nov 1921, 484. Similar quotes: "Mr. Ford Shows His Museum," *NYT*, Jan 12, 1936; "Ford Decries Debts of Credit System," *NYT*, Jun 20, 1926; "Ford Defends Life in Industrial Age," *NYT*, Jul 30, 1930.
7. Stiger, 33.
8. Garrett, 68.
9. "Mr. Ford's Page," *Dearborn Independent*, Sept 10, 1927.
10. James C. Derieux, "Faith in the Future," *Good Housekeeping*, Jul 1933.

11. Henry Ford, "Things I've Been Thinking About," *American Magazine*, Feb 1936, 107.
12. Ford and Crowther, *My Life and Work*, 101.
13. Ibid., 114.
14. "Henry Ford Talks to Young Men," *American Magazine*, Aug 1929, 158.
15. "Looking under the Human Hood," *Rotarian*, Jan 1947, 9.
16. Lewis, 79, citing *Ford Times*, Oct 1915.
17. "Henry Ford Back, Admits an Error, Denies Deserting," *NYT*, Jan 3, 1916.
18. Edgar A. Guest, "Henry Ford Talks about His Mother," *American Magazine*, Jul 1923, 120.
19. "Religion: Reincarnationist," *Time*, Sept 3, 1928, 42.
20. Ford, *Ford Ideals*, 72.
21. "Mr. Ford's Page," *Dearborn Independent*, Dec 19, 1925.
22. "Mr. Ford Shows His Museum," *NYT*, Jan 12, 1936.
23. Ford and Crowther, *My Life and Work*, 10.
24. Jardim, 124, citing *New York World*, Jul 18, 1919.
25. Ford, *Ford Ideals*, 27.
26. Ralph Waldo Trine, "The Power That Wins," *Theosophist*, Jan 1930, 180.
27. Bushnell, 51.
28. Ford and Crowther, *My Life and Work*, 19.
29. Ibid., 36.
30. Ibid., 19.
31. Henry Ford, "Faith," *American Magazine*, Feb 1941, 9.
32. Ford and Crowther, *My Life and Work*, 5.
33. Ford, *Ford Ideals*, 74.
34. Marquis, 14.
35. Stidger, 38. Also inscription on an autographed photo given to Albert Kahn, a Jewish architect who worked for him. Brinkley, 137.
36. Ford and Crowther, *My Life and Work*, 269.
37. Ibid., 96.
38. Ford and Faurote, *My Philosophy of Industry*, 19.
39. Trine, 28.
40. "Ford Scans the Economic Scene," *NYT*, May 24, 1931.
41. "The Promise of the Future Makes the Present Seem Drab," *NYT*, Sept 13, 1931.
42. James C. Derieux, "Faith in the Future," *Good Housekeeping*, Jul 1933.
43. "Mr. Ford Shows His Museum," *NYT*, Jan 12, 1936.

44. Ford, *Ford Ideals*, 69.
45. Ibid., 23.
46. Bennett, 211.
47. According to Harry Bennett, who interviewed the photographer, the image was not faked.
48. Baldwin, 301.
49. "Ford's Platform Out: 'No Place Like Home,'" *Literary Digest*, Jul 14, 1923, 36.
50. Benson, 270.
51. "'Happiness on the Road,' Declares Henry Ford," *Boston Daily Globe*, May 11, 1926. Similar quote: "Henry Ford Tells Us We Should Work," *NYT*, May 16, 1926.
52. "Most of Materialism in Poverty, Says Ford," *NYT*, Dec 17, 1929.
53. "Henry Ford, Dreamer and Worker," *Review of Reviews*, Nov 1921, 482.
54. "Ford's Sayings Reveal Life's Philosophy," *Toledo (Ohio) Blade*, Apr 8, 1947.
55. "Ford's Platform Out: 'No Place Like Home,'" *Literary Digest*, Jul 14, 1923, 36.
56. Elizabeth Breuer, "Henry Ford and the Believer," *Ladies' Home Journal*, Sept 1923, 8.
57. Ford and Faurote, *My Philosophy of Industry*, 5.
58. "New Era Is Here, Henry Ford Says," *NYT*, Aug 21, 1922.
59. Ford, *Ford Ideals*, 52.
60. "Henry Ford Writes a Utopia in Terms of Machinery," *NYT*, Jul 11, 1926.
61. Ford, *Ford Ideals*, 47.
62. Ibid.
63. Lane, 142.
64. "The 'Appalling Simplicity' of Henry Ford," *Current Opinion*, Nov 1916, 312.
65. "Ford's Advice to Boys," *NYT*, Jan 25, 1919.
66. Ford, *Ford Ideals*, 37.
67. Ford and Crowther, *My Life and Work*, 2.
68. Ibid., 17.
69. Nye, 68.
70. Ford, *Ford Ideals*, 65.
71. Stidger, 184. Similar quote: "Looking under the Human Hood," *Rotarian*, Jan 1947, 10.

72. "Ford Praises Jews in Talk with Editor," *NYT*, Nov 21, 1927.

73. Brinkley, 511, citing *Detroit Free Press*, May 28, 1944.

74. "Vandium Steel," *Boston Daily Globe*, Mar 31, 1907.

75. Grandin, 55. Similar quote: Sorensen, 13–14.

76. Lacey, 226.

77. Ford, *Ford Ideals*, 72. Similar quote: Trine, 62.

78. "The Great American Enigma," *Harper's Magazine*, Oct 1930.

79. Ford and Faurote, *My Philosophy of Industry*, 19.

80. "Education: Kudos Jun 4, 1935," *Time*, Jun 24, 1935, 40.

81. "Labor: Model T Tycoon," *Time*, Mar 17, 1941, 19.

82. "Henry Ford Defends Klan As a Body of Patriots," *NYT*, Aug 27, 1924.

83. "Henry Ford's Experiment in Good-Will," *Everybody's Magazine*, Apr 1914, 468.

84. Nevins and Hill, *Ford: Expansion and Challenge*, 270.

85. "Henry Ford Talks to Young Men," *American Magazine*, Aug 1929, 45.

86. "Ford Lays Slump to Era of Laziness," *NYT*, Oct 3, 1930. Similar quote: "Mr. Ford Prescribes for Europe," *NYT*, Oct 19, 1930.

87. Nye, 67, citing article by John Reed, *Metropolitan Magazine*, Oct 1916. Similar quote: "Ford Defends Life in Industrial Age," *NYT*, Jul 30, 1930.

88. Ford and Crowther, *My Life and Work*, 43.

89. Ibid.

90. Henry Ford, "Things I've Been Thinking About," *American Magazine*, Feb 1936, 197.

91. Bonville, 10, citing *Ford Times*, Jan 1917.

92. "Henry Ford on His Plans and His Philosophy," *Literary Digest*, Jan 7, 1928, 44.

93. Trine, 26.

94. James C. Derieux, "Faith in the Future," *Good Housekeeping*, Jul 1933.

95. Richards, 293.

96. Nevins and Hill, *Ford: The Times, the Man, the Company*, image between 496 and 497.

97. Ford, *Ford Ideals*, 34.

98. Ibid.

99. Ibid., 35.

100. Gelderman, 261.

101. "Mr. Ford's Page," *Dearborn Independent*, Sept 10, 1927, 10. See also Ford and Faurote, *My Philosophy of Industry*, 82.

102. Ford and Faurote, *My Philosophy of Industry*, 62.
103. "Ford's Sayings Reveal Life's Philosophy," *Toledo (Ohio) Blade*, Apr 8, 1947.
104. Lane, 75.
105. Ford and Crowther, *My Life and Work*, 134.
106. Ford Motor Company, *Ford News*, 1924.
107. "Mr. Ford Prescribes for Europe, *NYT*, Oct 19, 1930.
108. "What of the Next 25 Years?" *Rotarian*, Jun 1936, 6.
109. Henry Ford, "Why Henry Ford Wants to Be Senator," *World's Work*, Sept 1918, 523.
110. Ibid., 525.
111. Ford, *Ford Ideals*, 14. Similar quote: ibid., 38.
112. Nevins and Hill, *Ford: Expansion and Challenge*, 36.
113. Henry Ford, "Why Henry Ford Wants to Be Senator," *World's Work*, Sept 1918, 522.
114. "People: November 8, 1926," *Time*, Nov 8, 1926, 522.
115. "Ford Asks Dealers to Pitch in and Help Roosevelt," *NYT*, Dec 8, 1933.
116. Godwin, 10.
117. Ford, *Ford Ideals*, 33.
118. Ibid.
119. Ibid., 34. Similar quote: ibid., 35.
120. Ibid., 35.
121. Ibid., 44.
122. Ibid., 67.
123. Ibid., 72.
124. Ford Motor Company, *Ford News*, 1924, 4.
125. Trine, 146–47.
126. "Mr. Ford Shows His Museum," *NYT*, Jan 12, 1936.
127. Bonville, 10, citing *Ford Times*, Jan 1917.
128. Ford, *Ford Ideals*, 65.
129. Ford and Crowther, *My Life and Work*, 103.
130. Ford and Faurote, *My Philosophy of Industry*, 12.
131. Ibid., 21.
132. "Hoarded Funds Lost, Asserts Henry Ford," *NYT*, Nov 8, 1931.
133. James C. Derieux, "Faith in the Future," *Good Housekeeping*, Jul 1933.
134. Nye, 60.
135. Watts, 134.
136. James C. Derieux, "Faith in the Future," *Good Housekeeping*, Jul 1933.

137. "Ford Says High Pay Will End Slump," *NYT*, May 29, 1930. Similar quotes: "Automobiles and Soybeans," *Rotarian*, Sept 1933; Nevins and Hill, *Ford: Expansion and Challenge*, 610.

138. Nye, 129.

139. Dahlinger, 218.

140. Ford and Crowther, *My Life and Work*, 14.

141. "Imaginary Interviews," *Time*, Sept 3, 1923, 26.

142. Ford, *Ford Ideals*, 32.

143. Ibid., 32.

Chapter 21. Henry Ford on Others

1. "Ford Discards Bryan," *NYT*, Jan 16, 1920

2. "John Burroughs Dies on Train," *NYT*, Mar 20, 1921.

3. "Burroughs Funeral Today," *NYT*, Apr 2, 1921.

4. Bryan, *Friends, Families and Forays*, 68.

5. "The '43 Ford," *Fortune*, Feb 1943, 112.

6. "Ford Calls Couzens Best Pick for Senate," *NYT*, Dec 3, 1922.

7. "Banks: Michigan Moratorium," *Time*, Feb 27, 1933, 12.

8. "Henry Ford Explains Why He Gives Away $10,000,000," *NYT*, Jan 11, 1914.

9. "Ford Calls Edison 'The Happiest Man,'" *NYT*, Mar 7, 1929. Similar quote: "Henry Ford Explains Why He Gives Away $10,000,000," *NYT*, Jan 11, 1914.

10. Newton, 99.

11. Bryan, *Friends, Families and Forays*, 76.

12. Baldwin, 273, citing *American Hebrew*, Dec 1933.

13. Riefenstahl, 238.

14. Newton, 107.

15. Bennett, 213.

16. "Ford, on Air, Urges Election of Hoover," *NYT*, Oct 20, 1932.

17. Pelfrey, 250.

18. Ford and Faurote, *My Philosophy of Industry*, 3–4.

19. Watts, 20.

20. "Newberry a Victim, Says Henry Ford," *NYT*, Dec 6, 1919.

21. "National Affairs: Like a Dream," *Time*, May 9, 1938, 9. Similar quote: "Model T Meeting, *Newsweek*, May 9, 1938, 11.

22. "Ford Answers Roosevelt," *NYT*, May 16, 1916.

23. Baldwin, 66.

24. "Henry Ford Has New Peace Plan," *Boston Daily Globe*, Feb 7, 1916.
25. Leonard, 67.
26. "Should Build Ships on Standard Model," *Boston Daily Globe*, Nov 18, 1917.

Chapter 22. Others on Henry Ford

1. Baldwin, 76.
2. "Books: Mobile Vulgus," *Time*, May 12, 1930, 86.
3. Stidger, 42.
4. Barrus, 228.
5. "Sidelights on Ford and Edison as Seen by John Burroughs," *Current Opinion*, Dec 1921, 743.
6. Jardim, 34.
7. "Palestine: Oozlebarts and Cantor," *Time*, Aug 15, 1938, 15.
8. "The Serious Opinions of Charles Chaplin," *NYT*, Sept 18, 1921.
9. "Radicals: Red Hunt," *Time*, Aug 4, 1930.
10. "Henry Ford," *Chicago Tribune*, Aug 25, 1918.
11. Untitled article, *Chicago Tribune*, June 19, 1923.
12. "Couzens Ridicules Ford's Candidacy," *NYT*, Nov 1, 1923.
13. Dahlinger, 235.
14. "Daniels to Aid of Ford," *NYT*, Oct 25, 1918.
15. Wik, 221, citing "Poverty Makes Criminals," *Terre Haute Post*, Feb 4, 1916.
16. "National Affairs: Booms," *Time*, Nov 5, 1923, 1.
17. Richards, 158.
18. Pitrone, 54.
19. Conot, *A Streak of Luck*, 443.
20. Garrett, 78.
21. Burroughs, 336.
22. Marquis, 7.
23. Wik, 143.
24. Bryan, *Friends, Families and Forays*, 32.
25. Ibid., 35.
26. Gelderman, 210.
27. "Henry Ford Says He Doesn't Want to Be U.S. President," *Boston Daily Globe,* Apr 10, 1923.
28. Bryan, *Clara: Mrs. Henry Ford,* 185; Nevins and Hill, *Ford: Expansion and Challenge*, 303. Similar quote: Clancey, 159.

29. Elizabeth Breuer, "Henry Ford and the Believer," *Ladies' Home Journal,* Sept 1923, 124.
30. Ibid., 125.
31. Nevins and Hill, *Ford: Expansion and Challenge,* 276–77.
32. Nevins and Hill, *Ford: Decline and Rebirth,* 123.
33. Lacey, 440.
34. Watts, 4.
35. Ibid., 21.
36. "National Affairs: Problem Child," *Time,* Sept 6, 1937, 14.
37. "Gandhi Dissects the Ford Idea," *NYT,* Nov 8, 1931.
38. "Cardinal Not Impressed," *NYT,* Nov 28, 1915.
39. Laskey, 30.
40. Higham, 155.
41. Ferdinand, 240–41.
42. Wallace, 2. When Ford received the Grand Order of the German Eagle, he was told, "Fuhrer Hitler has always admired you as an inventor, but more recently because, like Hitler, you have spent your time promoting peace" ("Henry Ford, 76," *Newsweek,* Aug 8, 1938, 10).
43. Henry Ford Quits War Fund Frolic," *NYT,* Nov 18, 1918.
44. Baldwin, 200; Brinkley, 137.
45. Leuchtenburg, 138.
46. Wik, 39.
47. Lindbergh, 488.
48. "National Affairs: Problem Child," *Time,* Sept 6, 1937, 15.
49. Lochner, 1.
50. Leonard, 120.
51. Marquis, 4.
52. Ibid., 16.
53. Ibid., 166.
54. Gelderman, 211.
55. "Attack Edsel Ford in Father's Suit," *NYT,* May 17, 1919.
56. "The Mussolini of Highland Park," *NYT,* Jan 8, 1928.
57. Rivera, 115.
58. Stidger, 41.
59. "Will Rogers Praises Henry Ford's Common Sense," *NYT,* Feb 15, 1930.
60. Rogers, 209. Similar quote: Collier and Horowitz, 13.
61. Nevins and Hill, *Ford: Decline and Rebirth,* 21.

62. Watts, 187.
63. Daniels, 176.
64. Nevins and Hill, *Ford: Expansion and Challenge*, 485, citing "Carl Sandburg Chats With Henry Ford," *Chicago Daily News*, Dec 25, 1928.
65. "The Press: Smart Money," *Time*, Mar 28, 1927, 77. Similar quote: "Assails Henry Ford Here," *NYT*, May 31, 1927.
66. "Ford Gets Medal, Hailed by Schwab," *NYT*, Dec 15, 1929.
67. "Ford Stirs Up Europe," *Review of Reviews*, Dec 1930, 64.
68. Sinclair, 45.
69. Sorensen, 6.
70. Ibid., 27.
71. Wik, 4, 244.
72. "Wanamaker Is Skeptical," *NYT*, Dec 1, 1915.
73. Nevins and Hill, *Ford: Expansion and Challenge*, 118.
74. "Wise Denounces Ford as 'Contemptible Liar,'" *NYT*, Nov 13, 1920.
75. Grandin, 263.

Bibliography

Alvarado, Rudolph, and Sonya Alvarado. *Drawing Conclusions on Henry Ford*. Ann Arbor: University of Michigan Press, 2001.

Arnold, Horace Lucien, and Fay Leone Faurote. *Ford Methods and the Ford Shop*. New York: Engineering Magazine, 1915.

Bak, Richard. *Henry and Edsel: The Creation of the Ford Empire*. Hoboken, N.J.: Wiley and Sons.

Baldwin, Neil. *Henry Ford and the Jews: The Mass Production of Hate*. New York: Public Affairs, 2001.

Barnard, Harry. *Independent Man: The Life of Senator James Couzens*. New York: Scribner's Sons, 1958.

Barrus, Clara. *The Life and Letters of John Burroughs*. New York: Houghton Mifflin, 1925.

Beasley, Norman. *Knudsen: A Biography*. New York: McGraw-Hill, 1947.

Beasley, Norman, and George Washington Stark. *Made in Detroit*. New York: Putnam, 1957.

Behrman, Samuel Nathaniel. *Duveen: A Life in Art*. New York: Random House, 1952.

Bennett, Harry, as told to Paul Marcus. *Ford: We Never Called Him Henry*. New York: Fawcett, 1951.

Benson, Allan L. *The New Henry Ford*. New York: Funk and Wagnalls, 1923.

Berger, Michael L. *The Automobile in American History and Culture: A Reference Guide*. Westport, Ct.: Greenwood, 2001.

Bonville, Frank. *What Henry Ford Is Doing*. Seattle: Bureau of Public Information, 1920.

Brinkley, Douglas. *Wheels for the World*. New York: Viking, 2003.

Bryan, Ford R. *Beyond the Model T: The Other Ventures of Henry Ford*. Detroit: Wayne State University Press, 1990.

——. *Clara: Mrs. Henry Ford*. Detroit: Wayne State University Press, 2001.

——. *Friends, Families and Forays: Scenes from the Life and Times of Henry Ford*. Detroit: Ford Books, 2002.

——. *Henry's Lieutenants*. Detroit: Wayne State University Press, 1993.

Burlingame, Roger. *Henry Ford*. Chicago: Quadrangle, 1970.

Burroughs, John, and Clifton Johnson. *John Burroughs Talks: His Reminiscences and Comments*. Boston: Houghton Mifflin, 1922.

Bushnell, Sarah Terrill. *The Truth about Henry Ford*. Chicago: Reilly and Lee, 1922.

Clancy, Louise B., and Florence Davies. *The Believer: The Life Story of Mrs. Henry Ford*. New York: Coward-McCann, 1960.

Collier, Peter, and David Horowitz. *The Fords: An American Epic*. New York: Summit, 1987.

Conot, Robert E. *American Odyssey*. New York: Morrow, 1974.

——. *A Streak of Luck*. New York: Seaview, 1979.

Dahlinger, John Cote. *The Secret Life of Henry Ford*. Indianapolis: Bobbs-Merrill, 1978.

Daniels, Jonathan. *The End of Innocence*. New York: Da Capo Press, 1972.

Ferdinand, Prince Louis. *The Rebel Prince*. Chicago: Regnery, 1952.

Forbes, B. C. *Men Who Are Making America*. New York: Forbes, 1922.

Ford, Henry. *The Case Against the Little White Slaver*. Vols. 1–4. Dearborn, Mich.: Henry Ford, 1914.

——. *Ford Ideals: Being a Selection from "Mr. Ford's Page," in the "Dearborn Independent."* Dearborn, Mich.: Dearborn Publishing, 1922.

——. *Moving Forward*. Garden City, N.Y.: Doubleday, Doran, 1930.

Ford, Henry, and Samuel Crowther. *Moving Forward*. New York: Doubleday, Doran, 1930.

——. *My Life and Work*. New York: Doubleday, Page, 1923.

——. *The Great To-Day and Greater Future*. New York: Cosimo, 2006.

——. *Today and Tomorrow*. New York: Doubleday, Page, 1926.

Ford, Henry, and Fay Leone Faurote. *My Philosophy of Industry*. Dearborn, Mich.: Forum, 1928.

Ford Motor Company. *Ford Gives Viewpoint, Cautions Workers on Organization*. Detroit: Ford Motor Company, 1937.

——. *The Ford Industries: Facts about the Ford Motor Company and Its Subsidiaries*. Detroit: Ford Motor Company, 1924.

————. *Ford News*. Detroit: Ford Motor Company, issues for 1923, 1924.

Fuller, Edmund. *Thesaurus of Epigrams: A New Classified Collection of Witty Remarks, Bon Mots and Toasts*. New York: Garden City Publishing, 1942.

Galbraith, John Kenneth. *The Liberal Hour*. Boston: Houghton Mifflin, 1960.

Garrett, Garet. *The Wild Wheel*. New York: Pantheon, 1952.

Gartman, David. *Auto Slavery: The Labor Process in the American Automobile Industry, 1897–1950*. New Brunswick, N.J.: Rutgers University Press, 1986.

Gelderman, Carol. *Henry Ford, Wayward Capitalist*. New York: Dial, 1981.

Godwin, Enoch Burton. *Developing Executive Ability*. New York: Ronald, 1919.

Grandin, Greg. *Fordlandia*. New York: Metropolitan, 2009.

Greenleaf, William. *From These Beginnings: The Early Philanthropies of Henry and Edsel Ford, 1911–1936*. Detroit: Wayne State University Press, 1964.

Hamilton, J. G. de Roulhac. *Henry Ford: the Man, the Worker, the Citizen*. New York: Holt, 1927.

Harding, Gilbert. *Along My Line*. London: Putnam, 1953.

Henry Ford Museum and Greenfield Village Education Department. Collected Papers. University of Michigan, 1958.

Hertzberg, Arthur. *The Jews in America: Four Centuries of an Uneasy Encounter*. New York: Columbia University Press, 1977.

Higham, Charles. *Trading with the Enemy: An Exposé of the Nazi-American Money Plot, 1933–1949*. New York: Delacorte, 1983.

Hooker, Clarence. *Life in the Shadows of the Crystal Palace, 1910–1927: Ford Workers in the Model T. Era*. Bowling Green: Bowling Green State University Popular Press, 1997.

Jacques, April Key. "Inside the Crystal Palace: A History of Henry Ford's Highland Park Plant." Master's thesis, Michigan State University, 2008.

Jardim, Anne. *The First Henry Ford: A Study in Personality and Business Leadership*. Cambridge: MIT Press, 1970.

Jaycox, Faith. *The Progressive Era*. New York: Facts on File, 2005.

Kraft, Barbara S. *The Peace Ship: Henry Ford's Pacifist Adventure in the First World War*. New York: Macmillan, 1978.

Lacey, Robert. *Ford, the Men and the Machine*. Boston: Little, Brown, 1986.

Lane, Rose Wilder. *Henry Ford's Own Story: How a Farmer Boy Rose to the Power That Goes with Many Millions Yet Never Lost Touch with Humanity.* Forest Hills, N.Y.: Ellis O. Jones, 1917.

Lasky, Victor. *Never Complain, Never Explain.* New York: Richard Marek, 1981.

Lee, Albert. *Henry Ford and the Jews.* New York: Stein and Day, 1980.

Leonard, Jonathan Norton. *The Tragedy of Henry Ford.* New York: Putnam's Sons, 1932.

Leuchtenburg, William E. *The Perils of Prosperity, 1914–1932.* Chicago: University of Chicago Press, 1958.

Lewis, David Lanier. *The Public Image of Henry Ford: An American Folk Hero and His Company.* Detroit: Wayne State University, 1976.

Lewis, David L., and Laurence Goldstein. *The Automobile and American Culture.* Ann Arbor: University of Michigan Press, 1980.

Lindbergh, Charles. *The Wartime Journals of Charles Lindbergh.* New York: Harcourt Brace Jovanovich, 1970.

Lochner, Louis Paul. *Henry Ford: America's Don Quixote.* New York: International, 1925.

Marquis, Samuel S. *Henry Ford: An Interpretation.* Boston: Little, Brown, 1923.

Merz, Charles. *And Then Came Ford.* New York: Doubleday, Doran, 1929.

Miller, James Martin. *The Amazing Story of Henry Ford.* Cincinnati: James Martin Miller, 1922.

National Association of Power Engineers. *National Engineer.* 1922.

Nevins, Allan, and Frank Earnest Hill. *Ford: Decline and Rebirth, 1933–1962.* New York: Scribners, 1963.

———. *Ford: Expansion and Challenge, 1915–1933.* New York: Scribners, 1957.

———. *Ford: The Times, the Man, the Company.* New York: Scribner's Sons, 1954.

Newton, James D. *Uncommon Friends.* San Diego: Harcourt, Brace, Jovanovich, 1987.

North American Wildlife Federation, National Wildlife Federation, American Game Protection and Propagation Association. *American Wildlife.* Cornell University, Ithaca, New York, 1912.

Nye, David E. *Henry Ford, "Ignorant Idealist."* Port Washington, N.Y.: Kennikat, 1979.

Olson, Sidney. *Young Henry Ford.* Detroit: Wayne State University Press, 1997.

Pelfrey, William. *Billy, Alfred, and General Motors: The Story of Two Unique Men and a Legendary Company, and a Remarkable Time in American History*. New York: AMACOM, 2006.

Pipp, E. G. *The Real Henry Ford*. Detroit: E. G. Pipp, 1922.

Pitrone, Jean Maddern. *Tangled Web: Legacy of Auto Pioneer John F. Dodge*. Hamtramck, Mich.: Avenue, 1989.

Rae, John B. *Henry Ford*. Englewood Cliffs, N.J.: Prentice-Hall, 1969.

Richards, William C. *The Last Billionaire, Henry Ford*. New York: Scribner's Sons, 1948.

Riefenstahl, Leni. *The Sieve of Time: The Memoirs of Leni Riefenstahl*. London: Quartet, 1992.

Rivera, Diego. *My Art, My Life*. New York: Citadel, 1960.

Rogers, Will. *Autobiography*. New York: Houghton Mifflin, 1949.

Segal, Howard P. *Recasting the Machine Age: Henry Ford's Village Industries*. Amherst: University of Massachusetts Press, 2005.

Simonds, William Adams. *Henry Ford: A Biography*. London: M. Joseph, 1946.

———. *Henry Ford and Greenfield Village*. Detroit: Frederick Stokes, 1938.

———. *Henry Ford: His Life, His Work, His Genius*. Indianapolis: Bobbs-Merrill, 1943.

Sinclair, Upton. *The Flivver King*. New York: Phaedra, 1969.

Sorensen, Charles E. *My Forty Years with Ford*. Detroit: Wayne State University Press, 2006.

Stidger, William L. *Henry Ford: The Man and His Motives*. New York: Doran, 1923.

Sward, Keith. *The Legend of Henry Ford*. New York: Rinehart, 1948.

Trine, Ralph Waldo. *The Power That Wins*. Indianapolis: Bobbs-Merrill, 1928.

Wallace, Max. *The American Axis: Henry Ford, Charles Lindbergh, and the Rise of the Third Reich*. New York: St. Martin's Press, 2003.

Watts, Steven. *The People's Tycoon: Henry Ford and the American Century*. New York: Vintage, 2005.

Wik, Reynold M. *Henry Ford and Grass-roots America*. Ann Arbor: University of Michigan Press, 1972.

Wood, John Cunningham. *Henry Ford: Critical Evaluations in Business and Management*. New York: Routledge, 2003.

Michele Wehrwein Albion is a former museum curator and author of *The Florida Life of Thomas Edison* and *The Quotable Edison*. She lives in New Hampshire with her husband and four children.

❂

The University Press of Florida is the scholarly publishing agency for the State University System of Florida, comprising Florida A&M University, Florida Atlantic University, Florida Gulf Coast University, Florida International University, Florida State University, New College of Florida, University of Central Florida, University of Florida, University of North Florida, University of South Florida, and University of West Florida.